Published by Honno
'Ailsa Craig', Heol y Cawl, Dinas Powys
South Glamorgan, Wales, CF6 4AH

A catalogue record for this book is available from The British Library.

ISBN 978 1870206 969

The publisher gratefully acknowledges the financial support of the
Welsh Books Council.

Cover design & typesetting: Nicola Schumacher
Cover image: Andrew Isherwood, www.warmlight.co.uk

Printed in Wales by Cambrian Printers, Aberystwyth, Printweek
Environmental Company of the Year 2007.
Printed on Corona Offset 100% recycled paper made entirely from post-
consumer waste.

In Her Element

Edited by
Jane MacNamee

Drawings by
Nicki Orton

HONNO AUTOBIOGRAPHY

'What being a naturalist has come to mean to me, sitting my mornings and evenings by the river, hearing the clack of herons through the creak of swallows over the screams of osprey under the purl of fox sparrows… is this: Pay attention to the mystery. Apprentice to the best apprentices. Rediscover in nature your own biology. Write and speak with appreciation for all you have been gifted.'

Barry Lopez, *The Naturalist*

Contents

Introduction

> One cannot know the rivers until one has seen the
> sources, but this journey to the sources is not to be
> undertaken lightly. One walks among elementals and
> elementals are not governable. These are awakened
> also in oneself by the contact, elementals that are as
> unpredictable as wind or snow.
>
> Nan Shepherd, *The Living Mountain*

I have only been caught in a whiteout once. It was just
below the sawtooth summit of Cnicht, North Wales,
mid-march. The mountain was covered in a papery layer
of uncertain snow, just enough to coat its lips and ridges,
a subtle definition of its deeper muscle. Underfoot the icy
layers were beginning to weave in. They cracked easily.
Walking through, I was aware of my own clumsy footfall,
the crunch of my all too human weight. I wanted to still
the sound of my own breathing then, to stop it breaking
that frail pane between me and the gloopy umber of the
soil, more pungent encased beneath the ice.

Absorbed in our tracks, my walking companion and I
had been inattentive to the shifting pace of the wind, its
colder edge, and to the gut-green cloud that stacked across
the summit, pushing in a rage of hail. For a moment, it
seemed that all movement of air stopped, the temperature
fell rapidly, and within minutes, the storm was upon us in
a thick, violent rush. With no time to run for shelter, my
companion, just ahead of me, turned to shout something.
I watched his lips move briefly before he was wiped out,

and I too was obliterated in a thundering frost of stones.

Instinctively I stood still, forcing my boots into the ground against the savage upward riff of the wind, my burning face bitten by thrashing shards of ice. All outline, perspective, and definition were smacked out. I had no idea how close I was standing to the edge. Cut off from my bearings, blinded by the dazzling whiteness, the chattering throb of my brain deafened by the screeching wind, there was only a sense of my body suspended, utterly defenceless, but strangely, unafraid.

I don't know how long I stood there, trance-like, but I let the storm move through me until the hail turned to thick buttery flakes, then a lighter falling, until there was only the sound of dripping, crusts of ice heavy on my eyelids and my lips, water slipping off my body and the glistening rock. I stood there without thought or preoccupation, both empty and more fully absorbed. I was 'awakening with the contact'. I put out my tongue then to taste the frosty sweetness of the air.

These are the ungovernable elementals of Nan Shepherd's luminous prose essay on the Cairngorms, *The Living Mountain* – an essay which resonates deeply with the intention of this book. In her passage 'on Being' she describes the feeling after hours of steady walking in the mountains, when the senses are keyed and the body not 'negligible' but 'paramount':

> One is not bodiless, but essential body. It is therefore
> when the body is keyed to its highest potential and

> controlled to a profound harmony deepening into
> something that resembles trance, that I discover most
> nearly what it is to be. I have walked out of the body
> and into the mountain. I am a manifestation of its
> total life, as the starry saxifrage or the white-winged
> ptarmigan.

It was the desire to find expression for this 'profound harmony', the manifestation of 'total life', and this journey into 'essential being' through prolonged contact with the elements, that brought this anthology to fruition – an autobiographical volume of over twenty original women's voices from Wales, recounting their experiences within the landscapes which have shaped both their inner and outer lives. It is not a collection for lovers of speed or insatiable do-ers. No, it is a much slower project. Written in the aftermath of the Second World War but not published until 30 years later in 1977, Shepherd recognised the dissonance of *The Living Mountain* with the speed of her own age:

> It is a tale too slow for the impatience of our age, not of
> immediate enough import for its desperate problems.
> Yet it has its own rare value. It is for one thing a
> corrective of glib assessment – one never quite knows
> the mountain, nor oneself in relation to it.

It seems to me both tragic and predictable, that another 30 years on, we are more impatient than ever, half-crazed by electric noise, and our voracious desire to make faster connections to a virtual world. At the same time we are becoming more disconnected from the real one and more dissipated within ourselves. In today's obsessive world of doing, I think there is a welcome place for tales of slowness, and there are many of these within the collection : Hilary Lloyd's hours of fence leaning on her smallholding in the Welsh Marches; Elaine Walker simply stepping out to observe the world just outside her own back door; Sarah Boss' meditation on the Afon Teifi; Sue Anderson's acute awareness of time slipping away on a final walk with her son before he leaves home; even the studied observations on rock of self-professed adrenaline junkies, like Maggie Cainen, deep in her cave in Llethryd Swallet.

Akin to slowness is the 'rare value' of solitude and silence, valuable as Max Picard describes in *The World of Silence* , precisely because it is utterly 'useless':

> Silence is the only phenomenon today that is 'useless'. It does not fit into the world of profit and utility. It simply is… It is 'unproductive'. Therefore it is regarded as valueless. Yet there is more help and healing in silence than in all the 'useful things'. (Silence)…interferes with the regular flow of the purposeful. It strengthens the untouchable, it lessens the damage inflicted by exploitation. It makes things whole again, by taking them back from the world of dissipation into the world of wholes.[1]

I'd like to think the writers included here would be pleased to be associated with something so utterly 'useless' – just like Christine Evans' description of her impulse to leap upwards towards the brilliance of the full moon 'rapt and wrapped' in it – just because; or Martha Stephens' regular walks up Y Coity, similarly without 'purpose'. 'The journey to the top,' she writes, 'is never just a race to ponder the horizon.'

Of course there is purpose in the collection, but of a different kind : Barbara Jones' years of research into the ecology and genetics of one of Britain's rarest plants, the Snowdon Lily; Gwyneth Evans' life on a farm which has been in her family for fifty years; Jackie Davies' inspiration drawn from Dyffryn Tanat to create her paintings; Emily Hinshelwood's search for inspiration walking the Pembrokeshire coast path over two years, or Jackie Williamson sailing round the coast of Wales. But this kind of purpose has nothing to do with the productivity or utility Picard describes. It is drawn from that 'profound harmony' with the natural world which these authors are discovering.

It is often in their silence and solitude that the writers have come closest to what Nan Shepherd describes as 'essential being', a feeling of walking out of oneself. Take Jill Teague's description of mountain as sanctuary and ceremony, as 'a pact made with self to be fully present'; or Sîan Melangell Dafydd's first solo bouldering expedition as a child, arms spread out, mouth wide open, standing on top of the Giant's rock, so still 'I might even forget my own presence'; or Jean Lyon in Cwm Idwal, listening to the 'sloughing of the wind and the splashing of water…', and feeling that she 'was disappearing'; or Christine Evans recounting walking alone in the dark as something which 'takes you into yourself', where 'you move with as well as through the night'.

This experience of 'essential being', of living fully in the present, drew many contributors to recall memories of childhood. We delight in children's ability to be alive to the moment; in the expression of their unquestioning wonder; in their untamed enthusiasm for first discovery, of infinite and unsullied possibility – just as Paula Brackston delights in watching her children in the snow. Dee Rivaz's account of her life growing up in Trearddur Bay, Anglesey, sparkles with the treasures of her childhood on the beach, but aches in equal measure, with an impossible desire to return as an adult: 'And when I found my way back to that turning…I had to stop my childhood self raging out to beat with the fury of desertion. And I could not say where I had been, for it seemed to me that I had been nowhere.'

On our adult journeys into landscape we regain that same 'simplicity of the senses', an unwavering reliance on our intuition. With that simplicity comes a feeling of wholeness, reflected in the anthology by authors who have experienced the healing power of nature: Ruth Joseph begins to heal the pain of a lost friendship by witnessing the majestic flight of the red kite and contemplating its return from the threat of extinction; Kath Cuthbert, once a fully active walker, but now having developed MS finds a different kind of strategy for getting out into the countryside; Carys Shannon revisits Three Cliffs Bay,

Gower, healing the grief after the loss of her mother; Patricia Barrie takes comfort from the view outside her window during an enforced period of bedrest following a diagnosis of TB, and Jay Griffiths discovers the medicine in the hills around her new home.

The link between all the pieces in the anthology, is something touching on Shepherd's description in her final paragraph of *The Living Mountain*:

> It is a journey into Being… For an hour I am beyond desire. It is not ecstasy that leaps out of the self that makes man like a god. I am not out of myself, but in myself. I am. To know Being, this is the final grace accorded from the mountain.

Presenting this collection as something exploring the world of ungovernable elementals and essential being, and declaring itself as something delightedly 'useless' – did I think I would avoid the question of a gender agenda – i.e. why should a book by women writing on nature be so important, needed, or wanted? No, I did not. But I would not be drawn into a debate on the gendering of 'nature writing'. That is not what interests me here. This is more simply a recognition that in writing on nature not just in Wales but beyond, the female voice is not being heard well enough, and it deserves to be. There were over 150 submissions to this collection which demonstrates, that however few we were able to include, there is a rich voice out there and one that should be nurtured and developed.

And I do think there is a uniquely 'feminine response' to nature which expresses itself through the writing. Listen to what Jim Perrin, one of Britain's finest writers on nature has to say in his elegiac to a dear friend, Annette Mortlock, following her death:

> I love the way that women are, their difference, the subtleties of their approach, the way they move through the world, the things you learn from them in the quality of their absorption in the natural environment - in which, somehow, they seem at a lesser remove, more nearly a part. I see the men out on the fells, hurrying, hurrying, pressing through, acquisitive, eyes intent on goal and summit and the completion of lists, itineraries, records.

And then,

> ...I know the otherness of the essential feminine and am enthralled, become again captivated by all the knowledge that Annette has imparted over the long years of our friendship. How few the men who've given me any sense of this, and how special; how slow and sensuous in their loving response to the world, how gentle. Bill Condry is the only one who seems truly to inhabit here. I think of his hands uxorious among the mountain vegetation, the January saxifrage, discreet in their explorations; moments of vision flood in, of he and his wife Penny in their garden, the regard between them focused on nurtured bloom, he watching, attending, as the love flowed through her. Women's rapture in creation – their capacity to lose themselves in the natural world in ways that our men's minds disallow, from which we are kept apart – it is so beautiful a thing.

The pieces in this anthology reflect women's capacity to lose themselves in the natural world, to be absorbed, and at a 'lesser remove', inquisitive beyond the goal. Describing a woodland walk with her son, Sue Anderson writes, 'He is carrying a video camera. As an artist, he wants to record the sunset. I am empty-handed: I want to record the experience.' So many of these women's experiences are 'empty-handed', not intent on itineraries, without Picard's sense of utility, but with Nan Shepherd's recognition of 'a rarer value'. This is our 'purposeless' project.

My thanks in making that possible go to: the delicate beauty of Nicki Orton's drawings which illuminate the text; all those contributors whose work we could not include in this volume; the dedication and patience of all the writers included; the support, advice and invaluable friendship of Janet Thomas; all the staff at Honno for their indefatigable commitment to women's writing in Wales and their unfailing support; Phil Wulstan and my dear late mother, Maureen MacNamee, for helping to read through original submissions; Penny Murfin; and to Jim Perrin for introducing me to Nan Shepherd.

Jane MacNamee,
May 2008

[1] Max Picard, *The World of Silence*, quoted in John Lane's, *The Spirit of Silence*, p60. Green Books, 2006.

Walking Through

꙳

Christine Evans

It seems to me I have always loved walking in the dark.
More especially, at dusk; walking through from one day's
end to the growing stage of the next. Night doesn't 'fall',
nothing so abrupt and graceless: as Macbeth observed,
light thickens, so that for an instant colours flare against the
retina, then fade. Shadows clot into a vagueness so that
things are seen clearer out of the corner of the eye. At last
only pale objects beckon: an outcrop of white limestone
snags the glance, a new lamb glimmers, tucked in under
an earth bank; petals drift soundlessly from a hedgerow
rose. Sometimes – particularly on calm summer evenings
when the air is cool silk on bare arms – it seems darkness
seeps up through the ground, as if easing an aquifer, an
ancient core of black wrapped within the rock since the
earth's first cataclysms. It is a transformation we fail to
appreciate only because it takes place so predictably, so

often in a lifetime. We do not even notice it any more.

In winter it happens early and surprisingly quickly. I take a path my feet know well: up our sheep field behind the house, scramble over a stile and then through gorse and rough pasture past the cottage where the Pritchard family came to live in 1925 after their uncle, King Love, led the Exodus from Enlli. As the twilight deepens, things become first dark shapes, then outlines, and are absorbed, as if in a metaphor of all living matter. And the thickening air accepts the human walker too, takes you into itself so that far from other people's torches and fuss, you move with as well as through the night. There's an occasional rustle in the hawthorn as a bird tucks its head in, a whisper of dry grass that betrays a rabbit or a hedgehog's purposeful tread, but otherwise a settling into quiet. Soon enough, though, car headlamps – two, three, as if racing each other – will leap up and over the fields, there'll be a scattering of houselights and far below, the chapel windows glow, like long yellow lozenges, for a meeting of Merched y Wawr or an after-school practice for the Spring Eisteddfod. And then down the road home, the dog and I padding round to the back door, throwing it open to a blare of bright noise and the smell of baking potatoes. They look up – whoever's there - stupid with warmth and television news, and I feel an intruder, too big for the room, more real, charged. Fully alive.

I have done it in reverse, this walking through: slipped out of the marital bed in the greyness before dawn, pulling on tracksuit trousers and fleece in pulses of glare from the lighthouse, for my summers are spent on the island of Bardsey, two miles off the pointing finger that is the Llŷn Peninsula. Each white flash is less sharp on the wall, so when I get out of the gate, the sky is paling over the hunched mountain and the stars are disappearing, swallowed up like shellfish on wet sand as the tide comes in. But morning usually advances too quickly to get the feeling of crossing over: by the time I have followed the crumbling mountain wall up to Pen Cristin I can see my feet and the crouched shapes of gorse bushes, with the furtive shuffles of dangerously belated shearwaters between them. As soon as my shadow starts to throw itself on the ground ahead of me, I feel distinct, conscious of myself as separate, scrambling and puffing. Already, on this sunrise-facing side of the hill, birds are stirring. There's a guillemot churring on the rocky ledges, and gulls are circling and calling high above in the lightening grey, white tips on their wings catching first light like signal flags. When I turn to look the other way, there's warmth on my shoulders and little spiders catch the light and glisten, their webs strung across the bracken turned to fine silver. I stand and watch the island's huge shadow shrinking back into itself so fast you can feel the roll of the planet towards the sun. It is wonderful and exhilarating. I gallop back down, but not as satisfied as when I've been walking through the dusk and felt absorbed.

The habit of walking in the dark started when I was ten or eleven years old and circumstances forced my family to a farmhouse perched above the Calder valley in the Pennines. The only way of getting to it was a cart track winding steeply up through fields, straggly woods and then moorland, miles of its dark pelt rolling over the rim of the horizon past wild, witchy Whirlaw Rocks and beyond Stoodley Pike to Crow Hill and Top Withens. A huge sky, blowing bogcotton and forgotten Roman roads among the heather, dead farms that stared out over mill towns, sunk under their own smoke. It was a harsh landscape but I knew it, first out of necessity, then with a growing sense of connection. Our home life was fractured, makeshift: my little sister turned to animals for love and companionship while I found satisfaction in landscape and then literature about landscape. I learned the shapes of the hills against the sky, the slow motion gestures of trees, the clouds and changing colours in the sky that 'would move all together if it move at all' (we 'did' Wordsworth in Form 4) and I longed to be part of that unity. Walking at night, I found, was a good way of losing self-consciousness, or perhaps having the space to be more your self. Because other children, and even adults, were afraid of the dark, it lent a feeling of power, too. We lived remote from other houses: until I lived in cities and travelled through them, I was never afraid of what I might encounter. These were not great expeditions, you understand, just going from place to lighted place – walking home from school in winter, or after babysitting for Dorinda in the council houses. Running down to the farm because the milk in its white enamel billycan had been forgotten on the wall, or slipping out to look for badgers at full moon. The childless couple at Cross Stone had a television and would sometimes invite me: after an evening sitting in a row on their lumpy sofa I'd feel the smell of horses streaming off me in the cool night wind, and my dreams would be wild with cantering and whinnies.

Longer, more purposeful walks followed. As a student I sought out vacation jobs in places where I could indulge my passion for being in the landscape: summers at a farm on the slopes of Dunkery Beacon on Exmoor; nannying for a hunting family near the Long Mynd and a first taste of Clawdd Offa; looking after dogs on Tintagel cliffs; waitressing in the Lake District. Once I came to live and work in Pen Llŷn my life was filled up with astonishing scenery; I could do my walking from home and have hardly needed to travel anywhere else. In my first summer here, a teaching colleague invited me to stay on Enlli, Bardsey Island, and my fate was sealed. Reader, I married the boatman, and my relationship with the natural world moved up quite a few notches. For one thing, living surrounded by the sea and learning to swim was a new exultation: it's as near as most humans can come to another world, another element we can exist in only briefly.

Swimming with Seals

Somewhere far's a memory
of gills, a sense of being somewhere,
something, she has always known:

just as her life is settling into
womanhood, her story seems untwisting
to a dream of a sealself
sleeksided, free, somewhere between
indigo and singing green.

Blue light sinks deeper.

She glides through airless vaulted chambers
over a silver-mottled shadow
that moves as she moves, watching,
until she's not sure which is herself.
Time lengthens…

Then heart bangs, lungs burn, and she must
spin to the surface
while slower bubbles of her passage
prickle far below, fizz out
in an exultation of silver.

She will climb back on the rock
feeling the lightness drain away,
her body like a coat that does not fit;
hands opening on empty air.

I have only spent half-years on the island, though. There
have always been other commitments in late autumn –
earning a living, schooling, family and friends – and the
lure of mountains, wooded riverbanks, and estuaries to

explore on the mainland. For the most part I am happy within my own *milltir sgwar*, the 'square mile' of fields and gorsey headlands I know well, either on Bardsey or on the tip of the mainland overlooking it. However busy, my daily practice would always include a good walk or a wander – an hour or so, usually in late afternoon after work – until the day before my sixtieth birthday.

It was the last day of August, perhaps the last of a glorious hot summer that we'd enjoyed without being disconcerted by good weather. The baler had broken and everyone on the island had been out in the hayfield helping to carry a late crop, having fun forking the sweet-smelling dry grass on to the trailer, and dancing about on top to trample it down. Evening brought a sense of satisfied weariness, the body mildly protesting in all its joints, as I took our grey-muzzled Labrador for her last-thing walk. Along the cleared field, all gates open now, easy walking, the grass stalks like cut hair, and then up the bank by the old School and back through the bracken. Just ten minutes; I was tired. But what a night! Clear and cold, almost frosty. Too light for shearwaters to come sweeping in, screaming to make contact with their chicks waiting in the burrows, so the island was utterly peaceful under a sky seething with stars above the hill's black shadow.

As I turned briskly for home, invigorated now, there, suddenly, was the moon. It stopped me in my tracks. Full and serene, much more energetic than a mere mirror for the sun, the moon blazed silver across a vast calm expanse of sea. I had heard on Radio 4 that Mars was at perihelion this week, the closest it would be to the earth for another twenty years. I looked for and found its reddish twinkle 35 million miles away and just to the right of our Moon, and then – a real rarity, this, only seen on the clearest of nights, and never before by me – the rhythmic loom of the lighthouse on Strumble Head, right across Cardigan Bay. It caught my eye like someone waving a torch, signalling from below the southern horizon. There – yes, again – and again – a fan of white light opening against the dark and distance.

I suppose it was a dizzy spell, but I remember what happened next as a moment of rapture. In my happiness at the beauty of the night – of being rapt and wrapped in it – I think I sprang up towards the moon, literally jumping for joy. The world tilted, there was a surge of movement and wind brushed my face. For a fraction of a second I felt weightless, as though I might actually take off, as though the lift-off we all dream of were being offered. *Peter Pan* has a lot to answer for. Instead of a moment of transcendence, it was a foolish and no doubt comically lumbering expression of exuberance, followed immediately by a lurch, a reel of stars and bracken, a wrenching crack and a thudding into blackness as head hit rock. In memory it's all in slow motion, though of course there's no knowing what actually happened. I fell to earth. It feels exactly as though I had been picked up – and gone willingly, eagerly, into the sky – and been dropped, clumsily. The universe rejected me.

Bracken was scratching my face. It was dark, and the dog was pushing her nose at me in a worried way. I was lying awkwardly in a small hollow in the path, where a scatter of stones points the ruins of an old cottage and gardens. My left ankle was hot, and running fingers gingerly down it, that cliché of bad novels came to mind – *twisted at an impossible angle.* At least it wasn't my neck. Broken. I'd heard it go, and it was almost midnight and all sensible people had gone to bed. I tried shouting – in case someone from the Bird Observatory had gone out to look for owls or shooting stars – calling out in a strained sorry-to-bother-you tone, *Hello? Is anybody there? Hell-Oooo.* And then, sounding utterly unconvincing even to myself, *Help!*

The dog groaned, as if she was embarrassed too, but otherwise the night was silent. The smiling moon sailed on, the lighthouses flashed their indifferent, automated warnings, the light from the stars was ghost-fire, centuries old.

There was no more dizziness, but standing was impossible. I tried leaning on the dog and dragging myself along, but the pain of the limp foot banging on the stony ground was too intense. I had to get back before the numbness wore off or I'd lose consciousness again. And already I was cold, beginning to shiver, and my teeth aching. (Later, I found out that I'd cracked three on the stone that knocked me out.) So, in a half-crouch, with lots of swearing, I walked. And that, of course, is what caused most damage, together with the delay in getting to hospital. I know now that I should have woken people, radioed for the Air Ambulance, disturbed everyone (the noise! the lights! the drama!) and made a fuss – and if anyone could have told me what I'd lose, I would have done. But at the time it was enough to get back down the hill, crawl down the steps and on to the sofa by the Rayburn. Time enough to try to make sense of it, to get mended, tomorrow.

But eight days in hospital and all the skill of the orthopaedic surgeons with titanium pins and screws, followed by physiotherapy, calcium supplements and even acupuncture, can't make it so right again. Four years on, the most I can tackle, with two walking poles, is forty minutes or so of fairly gentle hill. Any more and the ankle protests, and often as not the right hip – the *other* hip – gangs up on me as well. I put it in these personal terms because – even more than the vertigo and tinnitus I've suffered intermittently ever since – the biggest change is an awareness of and even dialogue with, my own body. Laid up alone with it for whole days back on the island – all the holidaymakers gone by then, husband and son busy with lobstering and ferrying sheep and cattle to mainland markets - I learned at last to appreciate it. Racked with guilt at my carelessness, as you might be for damaging a car if it were the only one you could ever own, I took an active part in the healing, talking to the leg in plaster and tending it like a hurt friend.

As some children fantasise about being discovered as

royal – Laurie Lee in *Cider with Rosie,* for one – when I was young, I harboured a belief that the shape I found myself in was only temporary. I can't remember what I hoped my metamorphosis would bring, if I even got as far as imagining it; but my first feeling on waking was often disappointment that I was still the same. As far as I could see: now I realise that our bodies, especially women's, are constantly changing. They are not our selves, just our miraculously adaptable lodgings, and they deserve looking after.

Steer clear of rough ground, say the specialists, *here are special shock-reducing insoles. Sit down to do the ironing*, advises my GP, *we can give you a special slanty stool.* The physio tells me to keep on with the exercises and get a shopping trolley. My son sets up a system of tanks and pumps behind our island house so I don't have to fetch water from the well, and my husband buys a buggy so I don't have to walk to the jetty or the Abbey tower or the lighthouse. Everyone is kind. I try to take to sedentary activities sitting watching seals or sketching rocks at sunset. Not ironing. Each day I walk for a little longer, a few minutes further. Even on crutches I managed to struggle up the path to the shoulder of the mountain to use my mobile phone, but I haven't made it to the top yet. Perhaps this summer. I said that last year, and the one before that.

But worse than the physical restrictions is having to think for my ankle, not being able to trust it will sense when to avoid tripping or sliding, for it seems to have lost some instinctive connection. Not being able to take energy levels for granted, gauging them like a fuel tank would have come anyway with age, but most irksome is the first taste of being looked after: having to account for where I'm going, how long I might be. How would I know? I want to set off where the fancy takes me, and it has to be on my own. *But isn't it a bit late? Look, it's getting dark. Shall we come with you?*

So here I am, grounded. But flapping.

Hand of a Giant

❦

Siân Melangell Dafydd

This bit is not autobiography:

A giant went for a stroll. He was mountainous in size, with fingernails at least ten feet wide, grit lodged behind them made of small boulders and hair grease in a black rim. Imagine hangnails sturdy enough to hold your entire weight, a lifeline running through his palm wide enough to jam your entire fist. That's him. As if the Old Man of Hoy had cracked open his legs, uprooted himself, and started walking from the Orkney Islands to Wales.

On this day, the Giant found himself passing through the Dee Valley. He felt a pebble in his shoe, only he wasn't bothered to remove it straight away (his foot was a very long way away). So, he bullied on through, despite the stabbing through his sock. He walked on until he found a resting place and sat on top of Arenig. Furious by now and in pain, he took that pebble between his finger and thumb and flicked the irritating thing a few miles all the way to Garth Goch in Rhiwaedog Is-afon below the Berwyn mountain, and there the pebble rolled into an island of grass. I can only assume that in the sixth century, when the legendary Llywarch Hen lost the last of his twenty four sons in battle there, this stone stood in the middle, providing a blind spot, a shelter. Where the pebble landed, it stayed. Something eight feet wide won't be moved easily unless there's a giant about. Even the bracken won't go near it, keeping a foot of respectful distance between itself and the edge of The Giant's Rock.

Either that, or the ice age glaciers plonked that rock, along with some other abandoned figures, on an otherwise even brow of land. But since they exist there, in our way, we have a need to name our rocks and touch...

In the summer of 1986, we are three, all in our turtle jumpers: un-dirtyable brown wool with a row of yellow shells walking across our bellies. I nudge Rhys in the ribs and he nudges Tudur. We make a swaggering turtle parade.

In The Cave, there's only space for two. That is if we clench our cheeks, perch on a slope and rely on a bit of friction between rock and corduroy to keep us from sliding to the ground. It's not really a cave but an almost-cave; its mouth only. I wish hard for it to be bigger than my memory of it, deeper than the graffiti of *RH was ere.* I imagine finding something in dad's garage that I could use to tunnel, deep, deep into the beginning-cave and make it proper; big enough to fit my whole body, to hide and eat picnic. But for the time being, there's just about space for two and no way space for three.

My brothers, they bagsy the cave and bump their bums against mine.

I say, 'I bagsy it more,' but it doesn't work.

We have our ways of bargaining: who got to play Cowboy instead of Indian last, whose cake was biggest for lunch, who got to milk the goats this morning. I don't know which method we use today but I am elbowed and nudged and pushed along by the power of two bums. I dig my wellington grips into the soil until their yellow eyes shudder and I push back. I fail. My turtles slip rank. I end up with my knickers in a wilderness of bracken at their feet and my skirt in a puff. Down there, I have a green fortress and I make counting the leaves on one sprout of bracken the purpose of my whole life. I rip it until my fingers are sticky and alien-green. I think: this is almost camping if I stay long enough for the green to grow all the way over my head. Spiders tickle my knickers but I know that I can stand it. I stew.

Then I can't hear what my brothers are saying up there. I leave. Not even on a proper path. I lose that. Instead, I end up fighting through bracken webs strong as tree trunks up to my nose, seeds in my eyes, smacks on my cheeks and bits loose in my wellington boots. I know there is better rock. Somewhere beyond the top of Garth Goch I stumble into a sheep's path. A million edges of bracken have swiped my knees until the skin above my wellingtons are whipped white through the – what is it? Tan or dirt on me? – I'm not sure. I shake the scratchiness off me; spit and sneeze green; goo slips and drips down through sinews of red bracken mesh below the fresh growth. I look back towards home, behind me, which by now is reduced to chimneys; the rest of the house hidden by the Garth. I've reached the cut off point. One step and I will have wandered beyond where we're allowed, alone. I duck and the chimneys sink into the curve of the land. This is 'too far': seeing nothing but blue above and green below. Nothing else. I am beyond sight. I scoot along the path, staying hidden.

When I think I'm far enough for my whole body to be over the edge, I stand and follow the path over the hump of the Garth to where it evens out to patches of clumpy long yellow grass and patches of bracken rolling out in front of me, all broken up by twisted lines where sheep have followed sheep have followed sheep. And there it is, standing fat in the middle of a lime patch of grass. I stop as though what I see there, suddenly, is alive and naked and might rampage. Shh. Our nemesis rises out of its basin, dull, even in sunshine, the Giant's Rock. There, a plug in the landscape, protruding stubborn in a breeze that makes everything else about it ripple. My legs start running to it, downhill, through a wide sheep's path, faster and faster and furious, I run until the speed is not mine but a wild force that belongs to the thrust of downhill momentum, sending my feet thumping round, round, round. A speed that might snap me if I stop. Until I have no choice. The speed whacks me against the granular rock; my kneecaps and palms slap into place and shudder.

Looking up, up above my tiny hands, plump and flushed against the shreds and patches of weathered rocks, I wonder at their quivering. I am aware of bones inside them, shuddering with small muscles out of shock; shock and a certain wow at being placed right on that rock of legend. My bitten nails look limp as lace, but I grip until my flesh feels pierced, grip until my fingertips are pale and bloodless and puke-yellow. And with a certain fury, I hoist myself up to a waist-high shelf. The rock has a vanished skirting: foothold trouble. But now I pass the problem by not seeing it. It's no match for my bloody-minded determination. I pant through it. Go. Think tall thoughts. Cover the run of the rock with moves of my own and sounds of scraping boot rubber. I aim for a jagged edge that dents my fingers just under the crest, if I can just put three fingers on it straight away and shift my balance towards it and feel strong on my left wellington toe, hope, stroke, grapple, flap, smear, hug, cling, panic, no panic, yes I can. The rock's roughness holds me, I learn. Move quickly and my feet won't have time to slip off. A dimple: enough for three fingers gives me balance. So, my left hand reaches for the ridge and gets it. I finger along the crest for a safe place and almost as a gift, I find a finger pocket, a green and soggy one but deep enough to match for a safe hold. Feet follow. The grips of my wellingtons arrive at the summit first, my toes curling inside. I roar myself up: a mixture of triumph and disappointment because what I want is more. More ribs and raw edges, the wind whistling me like grasses, the sky on my back. I look upwards at empty air, willing it to be more rock face. My feet arrive and stand, four rubber yellow eyes looking up from the wellingtons with two tufts of grass growing impossibly out of nothing but rock, and there, I almost topple, body giving into the air about me, released.

Alone in the centre of the sky, I see its intense blue like a giant eye, bleeding to a blinding white at the edges, glowing from the summits of the Berwyn, the Arenig, the Aran. The land about me is illuminated with the thin sunlight of high places, sprinkled with odd sparks from farm windows and puddles. I watch the mysteries of down where I had come from; the fields green in their dry stone walls flaring in intense patches, Llyn Tegid gilded with flickers of sun and white sails; dinky cars. I am the girl and I am the one panting with the Giant's Rock at my feet. Far from what I think are the dangers of the world, I feel only a little fear that I am there at all. And I stand with my arms out, mouth wide open. I stay there, still, for what I think is all afternoon and is probably no more than half-an-hour; so still that I might forget even my own presence there.

In that pose on the Giant's Rock, there are some things

I know nothing about:

    – To avoid disturbing bracken, especially the seeds. They hold cancer in them, maybe.

    – That Chernobyl, in the Ukraine left toxic, inedible sheep in Wales. If drinking water makes sheep poisonous, beware of water in high places.

    – That hands will age a woman quicker than her face.

    – How on earth to get down from there. That is what concerns me as I put my arms out like a girl learning to fly.

Something glistens. I spot it, like a magpie. Cellophane on a pile of wilted carnations on the road's curve catches the sun sharply and blinks at me as if it had a secret. It is too painful to look.

My decision is to belly flop. I lean on my front and dangle my legs over the edge. Scraping downwards, I dirty my turtle. My jumper then lifts to my armpits and scrunches at my chest, my skirt at my waist, flaking bits of grey stone-moss upwards into my eyes and mouth. This is not time for an audience. I hope. I flail. My descent less elegant than my ascent. My wellington toes eventually find a resting place, press into it, trust it. From there, one, two, three, I say, 'jump' out loud but my fingers hold onto the one trusty pocket above my head. 'Jump,' I encourage my hands; they half let go so that I jump without totally letting go. I scrape my way down the rock, fingers still attached like a tongue glued to ice, all the way, the rasp of skin, burning.

I don't know that what I was doing is called bouldering. I call it not falling off. Only when I get to the bottom again, I fall off the earth. Nose to the grass and roll down the hill as if the whole Garth is rejecting me. I make new words:

Urr–urr–rgh

Comeoncomeoncomeoncomeo–on

Llllll

I roll all the way down to the tadpole bog. When I get there, I take a slurp to sort out my dry tongue, as if I meant to roll there. Bog water tastes how I imagine Guinness does. The sky goes pug above me and eventually I notice that I am grated.

I bring myself home to our cool cave kitchen and sit on the old chapel bench, kicking my heels against the metal legs. Daylight stays inside the square window and hurts my eyes, then my head. Everything is sticky. Flies stick to the window frame and flap without flying; my hands stick to the bench varnish, grit sliding between the fingers in black sweat. I thought I knew my hands more intimately than my own face but now, they have new raw patches and a new character. Grey stains from stone-moss and scratches replace my fingertips and shreds of skin hang like hangnails in unexpected places. Today, the landscape of my skin has changed. Waiting for dinner, I know that I have thrust into my hands the job of getting me places, the strength, the ability. And I accept, fingering my new marks into place like following a map route, I will scar. One piercing starts caking on me. For now, I keep my hands safe, tucked about myself and dirty.

I smell the out-of-doors trapped inside the knitting of my jumper, the twist of rusty bracken and squished grass, the curious nose-full of pollen and scratchy half-alive things, green un-caged air that could have travelled here from Timbuktu or Everest. Who knows where it's been. I breathe my jumper. Breathe and touch. I do not wash before dinner, like a lover not washing off a kiss. My faraway smell stays there through sausage supper and rice pudding and fades round about the time dad shouts 'square field!' and rounds us up. This means bed. I don't know yet if square fields are unique to our family or whether all dads believe that dreams begin outdoors, standing in grass. The field I sleep in is white and covered in Strawberry Shortcake, my brothers' are superman and cowboy. Before dreaming I think: hip left, reach round and up, three fingers on jagged bit, shift left, trust left toe, stand on that left, pull up and across, simple. Tomorrow I will return, with jam sandwiches and orange squash for the summit. I sleep twisted, arm up in the pillow, ready.

I wake up in a car. My hands are thumping as if my heart was in them. They cradle each other. They are clawed and covered in caked blood. Something has worn the skin from the tip of each finger, down to where the flesh is blood. My nails have been wrenched away to make moats of blood around them. Craters are left in the knuckles, gashes all the way to my wrists, weeping.

It is twenty years later and I have developed an elastic relationship with home, with Wales, but somehow I still seek the sense of the Welsh landscape, the touch and physical strength that means home, no matter where I go. On my right hand, a ring is missing.

What happened? I prised it off, the one I designed with mam at the Welsh Gold studio months and months before my eighteenth birthday, pleating, un-withering little gold daffodils forever. I grew around that ring. To get it off, I had to hold my hand in cold water until my skin was wrinkled, shrunk and shivering to the bone.

I left with one bag, remembering how my brothers wondered off mountain-wards sounding like goats with bells dangling from their harnesses, mam telling me, 'At least I have one child who doesn't climb.' This was not a saying; she meant it. It is a terror that comes from the same dark place as the fear of letting the three of us travel together in one car, without her. All eggs; one sport. She held the ring as if it was the only part of me she had left.

Wear a ring to climb and it could rip your finger clean off your hand. So, it's gone leaving only a dent on my finger, in California. I resist the urge to lick my hands and open the window instead. No jagged edges out there. A landscape made of layers soft as laundry in a heat haze. I suck in the one long breath I need to glue me back together, to be able to climb again. But for now I close my eyes, sleep again, warm air dropping on my cheeks.

❦

We are here. Today, my climbing partner, Steve and I are climbing the southeast buttress of Cathedral Spears, Tuolumne Meadows, Yosemite National Park. We have considered the sharp change from our camp at Lake Tahoe to this high altitude of 9288'; we have considered tender skin against granite and this is what we want… A moderate crack and face climb on what the book calls perfect rock. Not a difficult path for us today, then. No loose teeth. None of the pumping arm sensations that make my limbs look like snakes who have just swallowed whole eggs. Just phrases of movement and the joy of linking them together on a long rock face. Seven hundred metres and five pitches of commitment.

On the roadside, sorting out our gear in the car boot before the three mile walk-in, Steve hands me a rock-nut and points it at my sleeve.

'You have a feather.'

We get feathers. Quills and white fluff poke out of us like badly plucked doves. We find them throughout the day as if our skins had desires to fly.

He takes the heel of the rock-nut and butts the feather out of my fleece. Slowly, it falls. No breeze. Just listless heat.

We sleep fully dressed – no wonder – at night, it's cold enough to freeze our olive oil. Looking about my body, I find two more feathers. If I live this lifestyle long enough, my down sleeping bag will be useless.

I pick the two feathers out of me, check my bag for

water and Cliff Bars. 'Ok, I'm all plucked.'

'Ready?'

I nod and haul my bag onto my back.

'Grand.'

Three miles upwards over moonlike landscape, rugged tongues of rock loll on each other. The effect is remorseless: full sunshine searches the white ground. Not one nook is unexposed. Granite bowls cut by glaciers swallow us. The land is cratered, scoured, extinct. Our feet pit-pat from one to another: toe-taps hollering in a giant landscape. Sweat slides between me and my rucksack but the rope and half the gear on Steve's back does not slow him down. If he could sprint to a rock face, he would. We weave under scorched trees, their heads too far away to cast a shadow on us. We follow the odd cairn. We repeat the same foot rhythm, in convoy, and keep passing ramblers, climbers, one with tattoos of grasshoppers on his shins. We head upwards to the base of the peak.

There, words have been dried out of our tongues; we turn to our camel pack teat, and suck silently, and listen to the ground squirrels scurrying up a vertical edge, waving their tails.

Heat drags air out of my lungs and my limbs seem only half-bothered to be moved. But the first move on the first pitch sets me in motion with a sneaky under-cling. The rock is cleaner than my skin. Over the course of five pitches, I follow my marked hands. I become intimate with my new marks as if climbing seals them. I know the pressure I can put on some fingertips, and the piercing if I put pressure on others. I compensate as I climb and stuff chalk into a wound if climbing on it knocks it to bleeding again.

The more pitches, the better. There is something about committed climbs: spending the day together, connected by the intimacy of trust and rope signals, climbing ahead and coming together over and over and over, feeling each other's moves, knowing. On the belay point, we fold into duties of re-threading the rope and re-allocating gear, laying the pattern over slow breathing, letting the wind blow curls from our hair into each other. We nod in the direction of the sky at our backs and the basin of rock below; yes, we have seen, yes we have been watching, and,

'Climb when you're ready, then.'

'Climbing.'

On the last pitch, I notice the rope falling into a deep crack ahead. My body is eager; my hands recoil, scabs pulling. They will not want to be placed there. A body's cells have memory for movement. It's part of a survival instinct. Memory of a few days earlier, hand jamming up Hell's Crack in Lover's Leap: the gentle scrape as skin tickles the inside edges of the crack on the way in, the positioning, the firming grip of rock's teeth and fitting into the skin as the hand jams itself sturdy inside the crack. Memory of when the hand is cold, the rock colder. Sensation gone, skin rips and I am numb to it. No, I think. No.

I climb up closer to the crack. It gives no option but to jam my whole left hand in there, placing the hole in the back of my left hand against granite and holding my body's weight on it (for as little time as possible before I reach higher with my right and get higher footholds). No round route, no lay-away, no other hold. Skin cells remember, they flinch. As I expand my hand inside the crack, to fit; blood squelches onto white rock and trickles to my elbow. And by making this one move, I am at once, there in Tuolumne Meadows and in Lake Tahoe.

I leave a red drop on the crack's jaw and carry on, with a meandering stream of it down one arm. Blood dries and flakes off rock like skin.

The mountain's hulk reduces as I ascend it, reduces to one spear. I am heading towards it, knowing that I am running out of rock. A few feet from the peak, Steve sits on a two person ledge. He is hair and helmet over the edge.

'Lunchtime?'

I had forgotten such civilised acts but I climb harder, climb onwards for the sake of the sustenance I know I have, out of reach on my back.

I clove hitch the rope; he snaps in the screw gate. My other hand rests on the rock's white face. A small, sun-drenched, nutty hand. I see scabs but also newer scratches at the knuckles, scrubbed down to a paler shade of bone. Climbing chalk and granite grit highlight my fingernails and below, the rock glitters from the dark sparks throughout it. I almost don't recognise me. I am beaten. I am becoming a negative of the rock below me.

'Safe?'

'Safe.'

As I say it, he unzips me from the top.

'Where are they?'

'Top pocket.'

He digs about and pulls out a tampon. 'Blast! I thought you'd put in some chocolate sweets for me.'

I wish I had.

'Bad luck.'

We eat peanut butter and banana bread Cliff Bars, half each, ripped apart by chalked fingers. I wait for sugar. Chewing slows my breathing.

Then it comes. The heights of the head. The unutterable joy of getting here. I am leaning back on a single spire seven feet up, shuddering from exertion, neck to the wind, when brightness moves in. The ivory earth gleams. Clouds skip out of the sky and leave an iris blue. They leave me with a muscle ache that translates, even in this alien landscape, as home. Face to face with birds and giants, I have arrived.

Mornings are yellow. The fly sheet is daffodil and it wakes me by radiating daylight and heating up the stench of tent. How frozen will the olive oil be this morning? How much am I dying for the loo?

But someone opens the tent zip, hands me a bacon sandwich and a red-waterproofed baby. 'Your nephew would like a story.' A book follows, flung in.

I reach for the baby, both hands forward, and see my ring, and on the back of my hands, no open wounds but scars, purple ones which seem to bleed on the inside.

I remember a manicurist saying, 'Utterly botched.'

The world outside the tent is Capel Curig. My heart has hauled me home and this yellow morning is not Californian, but Welsh, after all. Yesterday my nephew had his first nappy change in a cave. Today, I will take off the ring again. My brothers and I will climb Spiral Stairs at Dinas Cromlech and, as I negotiate a traverse, knocking a fresh puncture into the scar on my left hand, I will wonder again, why on earth I do this. I'll take a baffled second to look at the scars clinging to me now like wet heather, fading to yellow, full of knots, like flies in amber, healing. And then, I'll plan my next move.

Finding More than was Lost

❦

Jill Teague

I was born on the side of a mountain in the Rhondda, in a terraced house that sat in its uniform row ribboning the hillside. My childhood years were spent on the vertical playground of these hills that I hardly recognised then as mountains. They were there as a presence, surrounding my world, accepting me in all seasons and weathers. They were where as children, my mother and father had played before me, building dens from corrugated tin and bracken, lighting fires and running home with their clothes tangy from wood smoke. To me they represented wildness rather than wilderness – riding the dun horse bare back through streams black with coal dust, where falling off meant a blue scar for life – the tattoo of coal; swimming in ponds brimming with frogspawn, bringing tadpoles home in jam jars and taking them back again under the silver sliver of a new moon. They were my escape route, especially from censorious Sunday eyes that scoured the streets for renegades – those who dared to work, or worse (as in my case) play on the Lord's Day. But to me the mountains were sanctuary and ceremony.

Leaving the Rhondda at eighteen it would be nearly another eighteen years before I was reacquainted with mountains with an intimacy as intense as that of childhood. It often takes being in the wrong place long enough to illuminate the way to the right place. At the age of thirty-five I took up fell or mountain running. I spent long hours following the fluid shapes of my sheepdog companions, running in mountains, especially those of Wales. And for a while I raced in them too – Pen y Fan in a howling gale, holding on by my fingernails as the red clay, frozen hard as granite, covered with snow. There were no race results that year – they had scattered in the wind like the Sibyl's leaves. The Peris Horseshoe in a thick, surreal mist, where human forms contorted with cramp took respite amongst rocks. I have been announced lost during the Carneddau Race, having foolishly followed a group of orienteers onto the wrong summit, and I have sat with others in the fields at Llanberis after the Snowdon Race, our skinned feet in bowls of water that slowly turned pink. Moelwyn, Cnicht, Moel Siabod, Moel Hebog, Moel Cynghorion, Y Lliwedd, Y Llethr, Yr Wyddfa – these names are like a mantra.

For me the sanctuary of the mountain begins with the first foot set on it. Like a pact made with the self to be fully present, being in motion on the mountain is like a meditation – it allows what matters to come through. The mountains strengthen the muscle of aloneness. Each experience of the mountain is like a microcosm of the life journey. It takes me to edges in myself. It brings me Mountain Perspective. Boulders, bog and shale, firm or shifting ground, going up or coming down – balance can be lost at any time. Fighting to stand on Corn Ddu where fierce winds will have their way, on Pen yr Olwen where rain is relentless and mist takes visibility on a whim, I learn to accommodate change, to be flexible in path and pace, to be resilient. If the way is lost, I follow streams downhill through crevices seeded with rowan trees. As part of the interplay of shadow and light, I try to experience the brooding lake and the one filled with reflections of sun and the sky, with equanimity. I find a sense of my own strength and fragility in the skull of a sheep or a shrew, the talon of a buzzard or a pocket full of quartz.

The symbolism of mountains is closely related to spiritual quests, to transcendence and transition. Over a period of four years I lost my mother and father and three other close relatives to death, both slow and sudden – terrifying in its randomness, and I was brought to a brink that I was as unaware of, as if I had been running a steep ridge in a whiteout. One of my father's last gifts to me was a new compass, as if he had sensed I would soon need to take new bearings. Death is awesome – it asks no questions of itself, only of life – how was it lived? How is it to be lived now? These bereavements were compounded by my own health issues, and I woke one day literally without balance, with my brain like a tuned out radio that insisted on transmitting and my muscles twitching and vibrating with the effort of every movement. For six weeks I could barely feed myself let alone run. The mountains receded from my limited world view. I was ill, dis-eased. I was out of focus with who I was in this new world.

Despite numerous exploratory tests no one could say what was wrong with me. The slow process of healing took nearly two years but when I was strong enough to stand and then to walk and then to run – slowly and with wobbling limbs, I realised that I viewed life differently. Death, disease and uncertainty had cracked open the fissure where a small light had shone, and now it was glaring. I decided to give up my teaching job and move home to Wales. It was at this time, too that I came to a cottage in the woods at Coed Hafod y Llyn. Cynefin is a Welsh word that is difficult to translate. It has multiple meanings – the place of our belonging, of our roots, our culture, our people, a place where people and nature are interconnected, the place where we were meant to be. And I had arrived.

In myth the forest represents elements we fear within ourselves, parts that are never entirely tamed, important parts – creative aspects of our inner world. We need to go into the dark forest. It might be a difficult and mysterious place - but fresh energies come from it. We claim aspects of ourselves that we have neglected to develop and become more than we thought possible. The forest was a final stage in my recovery and a new direction regarding my work and writing.

Life in the forest is heightened by having a minimum and living more fully – like a haiku. The cottage, once the old kennels, has a restored iron bedstead where an owl perched in the ruins. In dreams I hear the howling of dogs and the shrieking of owls – and feel at peace. I feel that I have found the fulcrum – acknowledging that up and down, lost and found are essentially places along the way. I feel connected to the raven's raggedness, the branches' bareness, the emptiness and fullness of the moon and to the blaze of meteors in a sky so dark. I find feathers loose among the leaf meal that lift with the wind, as if the will to fly could resurrect – and perhaps it can.

Not an hour, not a minute, not a second has been wasted on the mountains. I wear each ascent and descent like a row of obsidian arrowheads to mark my aliveness. Once again they surround my world. But now it is also the forest that lives and breathes in me and I in it.

I bring groups into the forest – oncology patients – to walk and write in nature. We start at the shore of Llyn Hafod. Taking time to reflect on where we are right here and right now, I read words of Native American wisdom that ask what we should do when we are lost in the forest. The answer is—

'Stand still,
The forest knows where you are.
You must let it find you.'

I'm so glad I did.

No Refund for Clouds

※

Hilary Lloyd

According to friends who dabble in astrology, my element is air. Examining my birth chart, they frown at rather too many air aspects and not nearly enough earth, water or fire to balance my personality. Maybe that's why I've always been labelled flighty, volatile, a dilettante blighted with an overdose of wanderlust. But it was my wandering spirit, plus a Geminian ability to build fantastic castles in the air, that took me in my late thirties to the Welsh Marches where the border winds between Shropshire and Montgomeryshire like the track made by an addled snake, or something with rather too much air in its birth chart.

In the Welsh Marches, I found my elements, including the missing earth, water and fire. I used them to build another castle, this time rooted firmly in the earth, and achieve a fulfilment I'd never found before in the huge variety of work I'd experienced.

I was to live in the Borders for a further ten years, building my dream of going back to the land, of finding a ramshackle smallholding with a few acres, a stream and a wood. There I would transplant roots I'd developed in childhood on bleak Yorkshire moorland but had left dangling through adult life. There I would 'settle down', something friends and family despaired that I would ever do, and live a simple life growing and garnering in the fresh air. Somewhere in that dream was the sound of wind brushing through treetops and of water tumbling down a south-facing slope. Fruit and vegetables blossomed, bartering formed the basis of my monetary system and young animals gambolled and pecked around the place. The sky, of course, was always a brilliant blue.

Thus, at the age of 48, a set of estate agent's details quivering in my hand and a fellow-Geminian and dream-chaser at my side, I arrived in a wide green valley straddling the Welsh/English border between Welshpool and Shrewsbury. The access to the house was a rutted stone and grass track that gave the car a free under-scrape and brush-up over its half-mile length. Two rusted and badly-hung gates later, we reached the property. Clouds massed and it began to rain. We were without boots.

During the next hour, we prowled, snooped and waded. We stood back and peered in, clambered over fences and more rusted gates then leaned against the few things that supported our weight to inhale an incredible view across the valley. It stretched between the blue-remembered hills of Shropshire and the purple-headed mountains of Wales and I drew it in like a smoker's first cigarette of the day. It made me as giddy.

In the chasing of my dream, I'd seen a few disasters described as smallholdings, and also inspected a few tarted up so much they had not only priced themselves out of my market but had lost their identity. This one felt different, despite the state of the property. No one, not even a head-in-the-clouds Geminian, could fail to notice the effect of decades of neglect on this former estate-worker's cottage and its land. We saw evidence of rising, falling and sideways-penetrating damp, bright emerald mould on the floor tiles, contrasting lavender-coloured paintwork peeling from worm-ridden timbers, and brown water stains on 50's wallpaper. Under one of the mildewed carpets lay the damp course, empty plastic fertiliser sacks placed directly on the clay floor. A sodden floor, even in early summer.

Outside, the fields gloried in waist-high grass and thistles. Hedges had reverted to lines of trees and a tiny wood was throttled by brambles and thorn. A gummed-up brook trickled hopelessly down the fields towards the house, not quite reaching it.

I smiled at the agent's coy phrasing: the property had considerable potential (very rundown), was suitable for extension (far too small), had a private water supply (laden with pollutants and bugs), septic tank drainage (you don't want to know), and adequate farm buildings (suitable for two hens and one lamb at a push, but not if you store machinery under cover). Instead I absorbed the important descriptions: 'this most desirable smallholding…splendid outlook to the south…idyllic location…land in good heart'. In my own coy phrasing, we'd found our home.

We made an offer that afternoon.

Two months later, we were proud smallholders with little experience but an awful lot of determination. My own Yorkshire upbringing at 1100 feet above sea level had prepared me for diabolical winters of blizzards, gales, frozen water supplies and long months without society or baths that I doubted I would see in benign Border country. And while the conversion of a town patch into a productive vegetable garden was admirable qualification for growing-our-own, the jump from a tenth of an acre to twelve is rather long.

It mattered not. We jumped.

That first summer involved heavy dirty work, mainly on the house which, despite the agent's description, was uninhabitable. The task was simple. The two-up, two-down house had to be reduced to its humble bone structure and re-fleshed. It needed a new roof, the internal walls had to be stripped back to the brickwork then waterproofed, insulated and re-plastered. The floor needed digging out and reconstructing with building-reg damp-proof membrane and concrete. Plumbing and electrical work would be the icing on the cake.

Short of funds, we asked a builder friend to 'come and

have a look'.

'Oh,' he said, waxing lyrical, 'look at the brickwork! Flemish bond, I think, and all the original lime mortar! Beautiful, wonderful, so *honest*!'

When we broached the subject of female labourers, his rapturous delight subsided a little but he agreed to take on two-young-in-heart-if-not-in-body women as his labour force.

Three months later, we moved in. We emerged from seven layers of wallpaper and clouds of old plaster dust. We had hacked our way through rotten timbers, tossed broken slates from the roof and hauled up new ones. We had collapsed nightly onto the narrow bunks of a caravan brought in as temporary housing and ignored our hairdos (plaster-filled hair plus rain equals something approaching a concrete wig).

We had survived the enormous physical input, leaping out of bed at dawn, downing a hearty breakfast before heading for work with enthusiasm firing on all cylinders. Our bodies had rebelled, of course. At times during those months, we crawled out of bed feeling sick at the thought of breakfast. On some days we didn't accomplish anything more strenuous than light a bonfire and watch seven layers of wallpaper and a jumble of rotted timber fly heavenwards in flakes of black ash. Then, exhausted with the effort of striking a match, we would count galvanised nails, make tea or simply lean on a fence, inhale the view and watch the sky go past.

We had also survived negative comments from family

and friends.

'Are you sure you've not taken on too much?' This from my mother after she heard of the heavy and filthy work filling every daylight hour. 'Don't overdo it,' she said, 'and I still think a flat in town would be more suitable for someone of your age, dear.' Pause for effect. 'Oh, by the way, I've talked to the family and they're amazed at what you're up to now.'

Doubts filtered through the excitement of my new-found life. Was I really too old? Was I mad?

After that call, I went straight outside to fence-lean and watch a whole hour of sky go past. And that was the day I discovered the soothing power of watching rooks swoop and buzzards glide through the valley or of tracing a meandering hedgerow across the landscape. I studied the clouds and found the shapes of animals and countries, or noted how they changed the colour of fields from emerald to khaki. Or I fixed on the dot of a tractor busy three miles distant and coveted its strength.

That hour helped me look beyond the present. It was a holiday, an escape into my favourite element – air. In the many periods of stress destined for the fourteen years I lived on that holding, I was often to be found outside, view-watching. Better than the stiffest drink, it would see me return to the house or fields ready for the next round.

My youngest brother was next to phone. 'How's things?' he asked. 'I've heard all about your latest venture on the family grapevine.'

I waited for the inevitable well-intentioned advice.

'Well done for getting back to the land,' he went on. 'I wondered when you'd get round to it. Must admit there have been times I thought you'd never find the courage.'

Oh blessed brother, enemy of my youth, friend of my middle age, ally in my oft-misguided moments.

I needed no fence-lean after his call.

With the house finished and our proper beds installed, we turned our attention to the land. That autumn was the wettest on record. Even local farmers didn't venture out on their four-wheel drive leviathans without leaving a notice of their whereabouts and an ETA on their kitchen tables. Our burbling brook became a white water river. The heavy clay soil we longed to prepare for next year's veg-fest turned to mud.

Mud was everywhere. It oozed and sucked, engulfing any passing boot or tyre in its sci-fi grip. Ruts deepened into slimy morass and the dogs stayed indoors and hugged the woodburner, afraid of being sucked into some canine hell. We plugged the worst areas of our half-mile lane with building rubble saved for such rainy days and marvelled at how quickly we'd adopted that never-throw-anything-away habit so beloved by rural dwellers and frugal Yorkshirewomen. As our rubble consisted mainly of half-bricks, the lane took on the appearance of a Roman floor. I even laid them in a decorative bond at one stage but the mud kept on sucking and my whimsy was lost forever to the underworld.

Part-time jobs continued but at home, what could we do? The house needed little attention until the plaster had dried out and anyway, smallholdings are for outside work, aren't they? We ruminated long by a blazing log fire to the sounds of lashing rain and the whines of bored dogs. Inactivity became the norm. I couldn't even whip outside for a spell of fence-leaning to lift my spirits. The sky had been sucked forever into a continuous stream of low-flying muddy clouds and there wasn't a view beyond our lower boundary.

'There's no refund for clouds, you know.' Not rural lore quoted by a farming neighbour but a nugget of youthful wisdom from my son on one of his trips home from drama college. I'll never know whether he was referring to holidays, or life on a smallholding, or just life, but it was a timely boot in the seat of my jeans. I stopped moping by the woodburner.

On our next trip to Welshpool one wet and miserable market day, we picked up a magazine aimed at the likes of us. It kept us absorbed and happy for weeks. First we read every article and feasted on details of rare breeds and cuddly goats, on the lesser-known diseases assailing sheep and poultry, and even on rural marriage bureaux (first essential for country courting, a stout pair of waders).

Next, the small ads. We sent for an armful of catalogues and happily indulged in all the ideas that had ever germinated in our fecund minds. We ordered seeds, envisaging rows of green and pleasant growth in dark crumbling loam, never mind the reality of the half-acre plot destined to be our veg garden, a weed-infested, rank and sodden piece of clay. The harvest grew in our imagination during those dark November days. Ripe pumpkins sprawled, lettuces of every hue sparkled slug-free alongside neat rows of beans, peas, onions, sprouts, broccoli and yes, why not a strawberry patch and an asparagus bed?

We mustn't forget a flower garden, we said. Somewhere to relax and watch the sun bounce off scented petals, or just to watch the grass grow. Again we shut out the reality, a stretch of suspicious looking ground and dog race track bearing only the remains of building rubbish and bonfires, and one forlorn broad bean plant from heaven knows where. (It died in December).

Next, the smallholders' supplies catalogues to plan for the future when we'd need hurdles, poultry feeders, ear tags, hoof and fleece clippers, environmentally-friendly animal treatments and a range of non-friendly implements no one should use on any animal. The state of our bank balance stopped us ordering much from these stores but we dreamed our dreams and heard the sweet sounds of frisking and baaing. It kept the relentless hammering of rain at bay.

In December, in answer to several of my yells heavenwards to 'turn it off', it stopped raining and began to get cold. And colder. The temperature took a nosedive to unheard-of depths and stayed there for weeks. The mud solidified. What was left of my Roman causeway cracked and split and ruts became things to trip over instead of squelch through. But my dark mood cleared with the sky. I could fence-lean again, and also work. I was back outside and felt I could do anything, whatever the weather had in store for us. I suspect now that water doesn't feature at all in my birth chart. Rain and constant low cloud depress me. Water, whether rain or bathwater, makes my skin crawl and my mood skulk.

I know now why most farmers are totally preoccupied with the weather. Spend most of your working life outside and every meteorological nuance will register not only on your conscious mind but also on the darker areas of your brain. It is too easy to stand at the back door of a morning and, while inhaling the view, allow the push of the wind or the slinking of a purple cloud over the far hill to colour the whole day. Worse, it can summon portents and premonitions of disaster and have your toe joints cracking in warning. After that, the only sane way to deal with the rest of the day is to go back indoors and tend the fire. By half-past eleven, of course, the sun is blazing, a breeze is coaxing up the daffodil spears and a headache, brought on by being too hot, adds to the general malaise.

We learned to ignore the romance of the skies, the moon on its back, and so on, and after our first New Year, the sun shone on us, if mostly metaphorically. Our water supply may have frozen solid that winter (and also our septic tank drainage system – no details, please) but we leapt into land management, gardening and animal husbandry like kids in a toy shop. I have never worked so hard as I did, or as joyfully. Fortified by several skywatchings each day, I dug and delved through the spring with intense pleasure.

Our philosophy on keeping livestock had been carefully worked out. We listened to other smallholders' and farmers' advice that unless fencing and housing are secure, the keeper spends the rest of her days rounding up strays and apologising to neighbours for animal trespass. A full year had been set aside in which to learn as much as possible about the stock we wanted to keep. Chickens, ducks, geese and turkeys would be reared on the best grass/grain/slugs/beetles then humanely despatched on their own territory. They would be food for the freezer, and to use as currency for buying skills and labour. Our neighbours would leap to dig our ditches in exchange for a nice plump organic chicken. They'd be queuing up at the gate in their mighty machines, fighting for the chance to cut our hedges or mow our thistle-ridden fields for a Christmas goose. Wouldn't they? It didn't take long to learn that farmers, like most people, prefer buying their meat from the supermarket in town.

Other best-laid plans also flew out of the window. One evening in our first January, we were heartily welcomed into a group of local smallholders. Jumped on, is a better description.

'Do you want any geese?' asked one couple. 'We've got a few adolescents hatched last year but our gander is making it very clear he doesn't want young competition around.'

'We're not quite ready for animals yet,' I said. 'Perhaps this time next year.'

'They're young enough for the freezer,' he persisted.

The next day, we drove over just to 'have a look'. The doomed flock was out in force. They were magnificent. Thinking of freezers, my stomach lurched.

'Those two seem to be pairing off,' said their keeper. The young gander in question lowered his head at us, eyes narrowing.

We drove home with a goose and gander safely boxed on the back seat and they never saw the freezer. They graced our patch for ten years, inspired our work, gave us goslings and were the best guard dogs in the business. Most importantly, they made our spells of fence-leaning even more delightful.

After that, animals came in two by four by six, mostly via cardboard boxes on the back seat of the car. A pair of hens arrived and gave us eggs the like of which I'd never tasted. Four more followed, and a small flock of ducks. And lambs, four of them, bottle-fed orphans destined to complete the family and fill our hard-working lives with joy.

Throughout that year and the eight following, our flocks increased and so did the work. We dug and planted and grew enough fruit and veg to feed an army. We heaved feed sacks, made hay without machines and regularly scoured stinking poultry sheds. We hauled bales of straw and upended sheep until our backs yelled for mercy. We even found the time and energy to build a lambing shed.

We also helped neighbours and they helped us at all hours of the day or night, especially during our first fumbling attempts at lambing. We survived diabolical weather and near-disasters, fires and floods and a hormone-rich ram intent on serving every ewe in the valley. The freezer filled and emptied with the seasons and our favourite fence buckled with so much leaning. Needless to say, its replacement was put at the top of our never-ending list of 'jobs to do'.

Working and tending land and animals is exhausting but being outside in all weathers in the 'fresh' air fed my spirit. Even the vast number of mistakes we made were soothed by a bout of digging or a serious though somewhat one-sided discussion with a sheep. We feasted on our life and gained rewards beyond all expectations.

We also learned the value of being part of a small community. Our farming neighbours – proper farmers, not 'hobby' farmers like us – gawped at our initial plans, told us in no uncertain terms that farming was 'no job for a woman', then later admired the results of our endeavours. We were known as 'those two girls up at Bert's place' (Bert being the former owner whose stalwart mother had reared sixteen children in our two-up, two-down). Neighbours ordered our eggs and called by frequently to 'see how we were getting on'. They joined us in fence-leaning, asked 'is there nothing you two ladies can't do?', and included us in their family celebrations. We belonged. Even a wandering soul like me needs to belong.

It was to change in 2001. From its hushed beginning,

the foot and mouth epidemic soared over our horizon in rolling black clouds of evil smoke that destroyed the view and filled everyone with fear. Trust and respect turned to suspicion. Neighbours treated each other like lepers, terrified of picking up the bug, even from a handshake, and taking it home.

We endured a siege-like status for more than six months. In our area, as in others affected by the disease and its management, social activities died along with tens of thousands of sheep and cattle. Holdings were invaded by officials in white paper suits, sometimes without warning and without permission, as ours was. And though our small flock of 27 sheep survived, our faith and trust in authority did not. I will never forget or forgive our leaders for the way the epidemic was handled and for the inefficient and bullying manner in which rural people were treated.

After it was over, we stumbled on in a valley changed beyond belief. It was little more than a green desert. Some of our neighbours decided not to re-stock and worked instead for other people. Pasture was grazed by machines instead of animals. Resentment brooded and suspicion still hovered.

I calmed my rage and bewilderment with good long spells of fence-leaning but more clouds appeared, those of illness and family dependency. We battled on for five more years but the spell seemed broken and our fervour and strength dwindled. It was with some relief that we sold up, to a young family who had also nurtured a long-held dream of being a living part of the landscape.

A year on, the problems we encountered are nicely soothed by distance. Sometimes I wander through photographs of the old place and see again our view of blue and purple hills and the green feast between of field and hedge and wood. Some pictures show the brilliant blue sky from my dream-chasing days. Others show clouds.

It's true there is no refund for clouds. They may have occasionally marred my view of the landscape and of life but I know I will always be able to relive our fourteen years on that holding and feel again the joy of being completely in my element.

Departure and Return

❦

Carys Shannon

The Departure, Three Cliffs Bay, Gower
31st March 2003

'Does this look ok?' My voice is edgy and impatient, 'Does it?'

'Yeah, fine.'

Good, I need it to be perfect. Today I can shape my appearance - today I am in control of at least one thing.

Outside the sun is shining, inside it is black. I watch the trees dance freely in the warm breeze. We stand, a small black mass huddled on the drive like a family of ants among the bright seasonal blooms. The dissident noise of birds singing breaks the heavy shared silence.

The car rounds the bend and I hear the driver politely switch off the radio's drone of everyday life. He steps out of the car, an impressive vision of solemnity. I wonder what it feels like to have to be solemn every day. My stomach twists inside me.

My sister and I get in and the car sweeps like a black raven through the pretty spring streets. Echoes of laughter, shouts, and children playing steal through the slightly open windows. I close them. Inside, a vacuum, a silence so heavy it pulls the wheels closer to the road.

I see the sea, shimmering blue and I think of my mother. I feel nothing.

I grew up here, I know this village. I know the ice-cream parlour, arcade, tennis courts… and the church. She grew up here, it was our home from home but now we sit like foreigners, displaced refugees looking for comfort. We arrive at the church.

Songs are sung and words said – yet somehow not enough. People come to talk but I can only return a blank stare and they leave. I stand amongst the passed on by the gnarled cherry blossom and touch its history, its years of life and death, a pink fluffy blossom falls on me and I wonder if it is a sign.

We speed through the town. In another life I would have added, 'And here is the pub Dylan Thomas used to drink at.' Cameras would click and I would furnish them with stories of debauchery. Today I look at my hands, remembering hers, like a map of hard work and heartbreak yet somehow full of love. I held her hand until it went cold.

Later I walk in a monochrome world as the sun shines on the beach lovers. I feel safe, the sea is constant. The dune tufts pass through my fingers carelessly. The sand sticks to the wet patches on my face. I hear laughter from a long time ago; happy memories float in on the breeze. It becomes night but I remain still, lost in thought.

I walk back in the dark, enjoying the unseen landscape beneath my feet. I turn to the sea and I see the shadow of a little girl who looks a bit like me and a lot like her, smiling and waving as she disappears into the waves.

I, like her, must now go home.

The Return, Three Cliffs Bay, Gower
31st March 2007

During the summer this path swarms with families, like bees in search of honey, they meander off towards the sea. A colourful mixture of children dragging lilos, long suffering parents struggling with cool boxes, lovers in search of privacy, a cacophony of family dogs fighting, mating or both and grandparents toiling behind, basking in happy memories as they suck the flakes out of a 99 Cornetto.

Today, the path is quiet; winter has sneaked in and brought with it a perfect, bright day. I revel as the wind stings my cheeks and whips up my scarf like a kite.

I know this path well and close my eyes for a moment as a pungent mix of wild garlic, sun cream and sea grass rushes through my senses. I haven't been here since the day of my mother's funeral. Instinctively, I look upwards to the castle and as the sun warms my face, memories cascade through my mind. I recall looking up at that majestic sight every year of my life. It seems smaller now. Further on I stop to take in the sweeping valley with its tufts of grass, pockets of sand strewn with shells, muddy river and wild horses who eye me suspiciously from their pasture. I can smell the salt in the air and at the horizon I glimpse my precious friend, the sea.

I remove my shoes and expertly dodge the spiky tussocks of dune grass before running through a mix of sand and wind blown shells straight into the river. The sensation of hitting the icy water makes me gasp but I persist, pushing my feet deeper into the current and delighting as the treacly, river mud oozes between my toes.

I wade further up the shallows, ignoring the cold gnawing at my feet. I remember my grandfather running down the tufty dunes with sand flying at his feet yelling wildly, 'Me Tarzan, you Jane!' Then he would stop abruptly at the river's edge, beating his chest before scooping me up and carrying me safely across the treacherous current.

With only a bucket and spade for protection I hunted crabs at this very spot, prodding the sand until amidst a murky swirl of water I would spy a pincer.

'I've got one, I've got one!' Squealing with a mixture of fear and delight I would watch as the culprit scuttled off into the watery depths. My favourite yellow dinghy often carried me across the water in search of pirates, the navigational skills of a child aided only by the strong rope with which my grandfather would tow the vessel from the shore.

The icy water shocks me back to the present and I run out to the safety of the sand, hopping to get warm again. I notice the water is a brackish blue today as I follow the river to the three cliffs that give the beach its name. How I love those three kings, guardians of the shore and host to a hidden underbelly of caves. I plundered those caves as a child, squelching through the bulbous black seaweed and balancing carefully on the barnacle encrusted rock. I would splash through the salty rock pools and search relentlessly for treasure or mermaids. Now I smell the dankness of the caves and see no treasure but only the way the water seems to hang in the air and the smooth, tide washed rocks lay damp against the sand.

Through the cave I catch sight the sea, today he is a deep blue, thoughtful and lapping quiet onto the shore. In him I see both myself and her.

Painting Dyffryn Tanat

Jackie Davies

When the royalist army passed through this valley in the Civil War they say its marching column was two miles long. It stretched from where *The Hand* pub is now in Llanrhaeadr-ym-Mochnant and wound up the hill towards Llanfyllin.

It wasn't the only army to march this way. Many have come in their time, from the English, who burnt Llanrhaeadr Church in the Middle Ages, to the hosts of Owain Glyndŵr whose home was at Sycharth six miles East. People still talk of Pistyll Rhaeadr running red with the blood of slaughtered soldiers as if it happened yesterday though, when asked, they're not sure if it was Celtic, Roman or Saxon blood or the blood of more recent combatants.

The valley is peaceful now, no longer a route for warring armies. It feels a backwater despite the main road that slices through on the way to Bala. I stand at the lane side and uncap my biro – biros don't run if it rains – hunch my shoulders against the Southwest wind and get out my sketch pad, intending to rest it on a convenient gate.

For a while I just look, taking everything in, planning the focus of my picture. But it doesn't matter if I don't have it exactly right. When I get down to the painting at home I can order the composition as I please so long as I have recorded enough information. And I can always come back. This view is on my doorstep more or less.

It's hard not to try and include everything, to aim for the panorama rather than the detail. But as always the mountains draw my eye. Not the high summits – Cadair Berwyn and Cadair Bronwen are hidden from view – but the outliers, especially the distinctive profile of Cyrniau. With its acute slopes and sharp edges it looks dramatic from the valley floor but negligible from the main ridge. Today its colour is changing moment by moment as swift-moving cloud shadows caress its steep sides.

Intriguing how the weather can make mountains look larger or smaller, protective hills or hostile barrier. On a fine day the Berwyn can resemble a friendly porpoise flopped on a beach, a benign, bulky presence under a kind sky. At other times, the summits shrouded in mist can seem higher than their less than three thousand feet. They can loom over the valley threateningly, their clefts and ridges dark with rain, or beckon with promise making you long to put on walking boots and explore.

If I had been out with my watercolours yesterday,

I would have painted the mountains with a big brush, let clouds and contours flow into one another, allowed washes to find their own way, sent my paint into free-fall. Today the mountains are clear of cloud, their outlines precise though softened by haze – blue-grey with a hint of purplish-pink ranging to bluey-greeny-grey where they meet the valley. I stare at their familiar shapes, almost licking my lips with anticipation. How will I achieve this shade or that? A dash of rose in ultramarine perhaps? Cadmium yellow with cobalt blue? This feels like lust. I can't wait till I have tried to fix the scene on paper, a brush in my hand and pigments at my fingertips.

But I am not painting, merely sketching and recording, working out the preliminaries for a commission. So I continue to look, lowering my gaze to the fields on the valley sides. I note a softness at the tips of distant trees. The top twigs look as if they are growing hair or sprouting mould. This is the first hint of spring buds, and tells me the season for mapping winter trees is passing. Now is my last chance till autumn to savour the intricate pattern of bare twigs and branches, catch distant views through their tracery. Soon there will be spring greens to relish and a softer landscape.

I note the upward curve of twigs that makes ash trees look like living candelabra, the delicate capillary-thin twigs of beech, so attenuated and hard to capture, the twisted trunks of hawthorns, bent by the wind, the solid strength of oaks. I contemplate the bare brown hedgerows, dotted white here and there where the blackthorn is coming into flower. My mind reels forward to May when the valley will be a riot of hawthorn blossom, the pastures criss-crossed with lines of foam-headed trees like lace on a green tablecloth.

The oaks that line the lane are old, their bare limbs torn by recent storms. I decide to frame my view with one of them and change position, abandoning the gate for a less inviting perch halfway up a bank. It's uncomfortable and I can't stay there long. I begin to draw, working swiftly in bold lines, anxious to catch the view and get the proportions right but careful to keep my footing. Soon the page is full. Ballpoint isn't the perfect medium but it doesn't smudge and you can get things down fast without worrying about losing definition if your hand rubs the paper.

I don't usually paint outdoors. I'm a messy worker under pressure and an amateur. I need space to spread myself and a modicum of comfort. I drop the caps off tubes of water colour and lose them in the grass. I marinate dying insects in my washes. My neck and ears make an inviting target for midges. I prefer to draw and take notes then paint indoors at leisure. As I work I write the names of colours on the sketch, suggesting which to use – burnt umber and yellow ochre here, ultramarine and Paynes grey there. I describe what I see – pale yellowy-pinky-buff grasses, greeny-black Scots pines with touches of paler green, amethyst and blue mountains fading to blue-grey. I note shade with cross-hatching, suggest the lie of the grass, put in arrows to show wind direction or the angle of the sun, add comments – 'this field disappears over the edge of the hill – next band of green lower so lighter,' 'violets here,' and so on. All this will recall what I have seen and inform the final picture.

But it's the moments, minutes, hours even, spent looking that are most important. I try to print a scene on my mind, enjoy it, absorb it, take it into myself. If I have a camera to hand I may use it to record detail but I prefer to paint what my eye sees even if the proportions aren't exactly right – long views can look flatter and more compressed when photographed. I'm not aiming for total accuracy but for a sense of place, a feel of the valley and the surrounding hills, the sky, the weather, a sense of the district I have grown to know and love these last six years.

Landscape painting is like painting a portrait. You can do a map of a face, a two-dimensional plan, and get a visual likeness but you need something more to catch the person beneath. Even a knowledge of bone structure and muscle isn't enough. I am aware of the make-up of this landscape as I draw. I have got to know its bones, its geology and soil structure, the effects of glaciation and the fall of its rivers. I know from our geology map back home the rocks that underlie this area: the grey Ordovician sandstone, perfect backdrop to Pistyll Rhaeadr in spate; the slate at Llangynog, where old quarries make an absorbing study in sombre colours and abstract shapes, the volcanic sills on the Berwyn, the acid loam that turns my hydrangeas blue.

But there is more. The character, the temper, the history

of the place and those who've peopled it over the centuries make the Tanat valley what it is today. I can't forget those stories of marching armies and bloodshed, the struggles of upland farmers with their yearly harvest of lambs, the holy wells and settlements, the squat, stone farmhouses huddled against the hillsides, the worked-out quarries and closed railway, the rich intermingling of English and Welsh cultures, the two languages, one surviving against all odds and flourishing so strongly close to the border. These make up the essence of where I live and are inseparable from the landscape. Natural beauty, even grandeur, is here in abundance but it harbours toil and celebration alike, hardship and wealth, dogged independence and human need, neighbourliness and isolation. 'We are so lucky to live here,' we say, 'even if it's hard at times.'

As I analyse the view I am aware of modern battles – campaigns to save local schools, dairy farmers' struggles with TB, the energy and commitment needed to wrest a living from hill farms and tourism. The valley's economy bore the consequences if not the ravages of foot and mouth in 2001. Now sheep farmers face losses because of measures following the recent outbreak. All is not perfect in Eden. Plastic bags flutter in hedge bottoms, winter farm yards flow with mud, basic services can fail and lambs can die from foxes or cold weather.

How to get all this in a painting? Maybe I'm asking too much. But if I can put my love in it, if I can add, as I paint, my prayers to those of Melangell who made a hermitage in a hidden valley in these mountains and sheltered a hunted hare, if I can express my own joy in this special landscape, my respect for the history and uniqueness of this border valley and my gratitude for its welcome, I may be able to bless it as it has blessed me, tell its story, capture it with paint.

Lloydia serotina:
Life on the Edge

❦

Barbara Jones

Suddenly, being deposited ten feet back down at the base of the cliff with my handhold still firmly clutched in my right hand was not what I had expected or wanted. The cliff had shrugged us both off, me and the handhold, to a painful landing. Whilst contemplating my next move, the feeling came upon me that I wasn't alone. But, who else would be in this remote, seldom visited part of Snowdonia? Looking around, I slowly became aware of a number of black shapes on the surrounding rocks, high and low, ranged almost in a semi-circle around me. There must have been eight or nine of them, hunched up and staring intently at this human form sitting on the ground. Death's harbingers? Was this the end or was I being fanciful? Of course I was. I'm a scientist and seldom taken to flights of fancy and it only took a second or two to recognise that I was almost surrounded by a group of my great mountain friend, the

Raven. Perhaps they were tired of a diet of dead sheep and small mammals and thought I was soon to be fair game or possibly (and nice to think) they were looking out for me as a potential comrade – after all, I am coming back as a raven or chough in my next life. It is an eerie feeling to have sixteen pairs of eyes all focussed on your every move, so I got up self-consciously and busied myself in limping around my perch on a shelf of land above the valley floor, hoping that they would soon leave their perches and find another potential food source.

Here I am high in the Welsh mountains, not climbing to the summits, but researching the ecology and genetics of one of the rarest plants in Britain, the Snowdon lily. This is no member of a flowery meadow though. No locations in a flat meadow landscape or a southern heath for this survivor. Only the steepest, coldest, most exposed mountain cliffs will do as a habitat for a plant which is so delicate looking that you would think it couldn't even survive in a greenhouse. In fact it survives much better on these exposed cliffs than under cultivation and most botanic gardens and gardeners have given up on its domestic possibilities years ago.

So what is the attraction of studying this and other plants of the mountains? If the cold and wet weather, loose rock, long walks with a heavy load, bruises in unmentionable places are all accompaniments to a life of mountain botany, why do it? I often have to spend hours suspended from a rope, taking notes with numb, cold fingers and trying not to drop anything down the cliff face as I survey these mountain plants. Sometimes I arrive at the bottom of the cliff vowing my next research will be into desert ecology. Why not chose a nice rich meadow with 100's of species and somewhere comfortable to sit? Well, I could cite the wonderful plants and superb scenery as rewards after the sheer physical effort of getting to and studying these gems hidden away in our generally botanically impoverished hills. There is also the satisfaction of learning new things about the biology and ecology of these plants and their environment. These are all important, but there is more. I am a scientist, but it is partly the non-scientific part of me which relishes the challenges and the pleasures of studying these plants - the part which is a climber and mountaineer and which identifies with and almost shares the attractions and trials of coping with this environment. These tough little plants look so fragile, but they cope with and have adapted superbly to their environment, just as I try to cope with and adapt to the mountains in which I work and play.

These plants aren't there because they can't grow anywhere else, but because they have adapted to what we consider a hostile environment. Most of them hug the rocks or the ground to keep out of the wind and have a cushion shape to retain heat and allow slow growth from one year to the next. The Snowdon lily, however, is a bulbous plant which cheekily pokes its slender stem and grass like leaves up out of cracks in the rock as if challenging the wind and rain to do their best to dislodge it. The single white flower looks similarly delicate, but this plant occupies some of the most hostile mountain terrain in Britain on north facing, cold, wet cliffs where it has hung on for at least 10,000 years since the last retreat of the glaciers. This is in contrast to its habitat in many other parts of the world, where it grows on sunny, rolling alpine tundra and copes with bitterly cold conditions during the winter months.

Studying these plants is fascinating and hopefully, will eventually help us to understand how to conserve them through the challenges of climate change. This is a tough challenge for plants growing right on the edge of their range; plants normally adapted to extremes of cold at high altitudes or latitudes. How will they respond to rising temperatures and possibly increasing wetness? In the UK the Snowdon lily is only found on a very few high cliff sites in Snowdonia and has nowhere else to go if conditions become too unsuitable. Should we care? After all it is found in abundance in many other mountain ranges of the world. In one gully in Mongolia, I once saw more Snowdon lilies than occur in the whole of Wales – in one gully – how many more of those must there be?

I think we should care. On a scientific basis, plants and animals on the edge of their range are often special and can have attributes and adaptations which don't occur in individuals in the centre of their range. These differences are the stuff of evolution and if we lose these, then we lose an important part of the variety and diversity of life and of future possibilities. They are also the pit canaries of modern times – an early warning that things may not be quite right. We should also care on a personal basis. Conservation is important on an individual as well as a global level and the loss of something like the Snowdon lily in Wales would be extremely sad for many people as it is more than an edge-of-range species, it represents something special to them and to their perception of the mountain environment in Snowdonia.

Even the scientific name **Lloydia serotina**, is important in the Welsh context as it is named after the first person to discover it in Wales. Edward Llwyd, a botanist and polymath discovered this small, bulbous plant growing on high rocks in Snowdonia in 1682 and it was later named after him. The discovery stimulated interest in the plant in the eighteenth century when a number of intrepid botanists braved the then relatively unknown and challenging Welsh mountains to find it. Records of botanists nearly losing their lives on the '*summits where it grows wild*' (Salisbury) or on the cliffs: '*...others held fast to the other end of the rope, he lowered himself down the face of the cliff and reappeared a few minutes later with a few specimens held in his mouth and more in his hat*' (Jones), show the risks these men were prepared to take to find this rare plant. Unfortunately, they were not there to record and admire the lily *in situ*, but to collect for their own personal herbaria. Records of 'basketfuls' being collected still send shivers down my spine, as does the account of a vase full of Snowdon lily plants decorating the dinner table at the hotel where many of these intrepid explorers lodged! It is easy to criticise these actions from our 21st century perspective, but these explorers did not know that their activities would contribute to the rarity of the species in Wales. Indeed plant collecting was all the rage in the 18th and 19th centuries, with local guides being employed to take the botanists to the best sites and, if this was not possible, to sell samples of the plants which they had collected themselves!

In the UK, the Snowdon lily is only found on a few cliffs in Snowdonia; confined by collecting in the past and heavy sheep grazing in the present. These cliffs represent some of the sites in the UK least affected by man. We have modified and tamed most of the land in one way or another, but generally cliffs are affected only by airborne pollution making them more 'natural' than most other places. So much of our conservation is 'gardening' where we manage a habitat for one or more species, but the few mountain plants we have in the UK have so far managed to grow without our intervention. The challenge is to keep this the case and stop things getting to the state where 'gardening' is needed. What could we do; plant the Snowdon lily further north where it could become the Ben Nevis lily? A sad thought.

It is abundant in many mountain ranges of the world, such as the European Alps and the Rocky Mountains of North America, where my studies have focussed on how the Welsh plants compare with its more abundant, distant cousins. Working in the Welsh mountains has its fair share of difficulties, mainly due to cold and wet weather, but research abroad can present challenges of a different sort. On Vancouver Island I was faced with a bear in the forest just at the beginning of a search on one mountain. What do you do? I followed all the text book instructions, I tried to look big (not easy for me), didn't turn my back and made no threatening movements. Then what? After about 10 minutes of this, the bear stood up on its hind legs, took a good look and then ambled off, probably deciding I wasn't worth the effort. Neither was my search that day as, despite coping with glaciers, crevasses and bad weather, no lilies were found. Other challenges threatening to halt survey work include a lightning storm which literally shook the ground on a mountain in Wyoming, Elk eating my samples, a foot of snow obscuring survey plots and food poisoning in the Polish Tatra Mountains. This may all seem like hard, unpleasant work, but I like to think of it more as a challenge to visit a distant friend, one who has a fascinating story to tell and I feel privileged to be unravelling that story which has been hidden for all these 1000's of years in the Welsh mountains.

I am particularly interested in studying the genetics of these plants. To most people, including me at one time, genetics is a subject to avoid, seemingly too mathematical and complex. In recent years, however, it has been used to study the history of evolution and migration of many plants in Britain. This produces some fascinating results and works like a detective story. Consider the Snowdon lily. Why is it only found in Snowdonia in Britain when most alpines are found in greater numbers in Scotland? Why isn't it in Scandinavia? Do our plants relate to their nearest neighbours in France and if so how different are they to them? Did our plants survive here during the last ice age? All these questions and more can be addressed by research including genetic methods to give answers which can really help in our attempts at conservation. I do sometimes feel a little guilty though. I consider *Lloydia* (the latin name for the Snowdon lily and one I use affectionately) as my friend and it can occasionally feel intrusive to be dissecting its every secret and studying everything from its sexual habits to its distant ancestry. However, it doesn't give in easily and retains some of its mystery by refusing to allow me to grow it successfully. I know few plants which are more difficult to grow. Most botanic gardens have given up and I know of only one specialist nursery in Britain which has been successful in recent years.

These years of work and play in mountains all over the world see me see-sawing in my approach to conservation in the Welsh hills. Often when I return from a trip abroad, particularly if I've been doing some fieldwork in the European Alps or the Rocky Mountains in the USA, for the first few days I see the British hills in a different perspective. They seem depauperate, over-managed and subdued. The ice ages removed much of our flora and our island status has cut us off from most immigration of new plant species from the continent. This has combined with years of heavy sheep grazing in the uplands which has removed much of the remaining interest (except on the inaccessible cliffs) leaving range after range of 'bare' hills with only isolated islands of a more natural vegetation. Look at many of the hills of Wales, the Lake District or the Pennines; several of our treasured landscapes are far from natural and as an ecologist I sometimes despair at the lack of trees, scrub, heath and specialist mountain plants. Despair quickly turns to delight, however, when I do find a copse of stunted hawthorn high on a hill or a clump of saxifrages growing out of a rock outcrop. The little we have becomes even more precious and makes me even more determined to protect them and increase their numbers.

I don't consider that we have 'wilderness' in Britain any longer. Some places are wilder than others and the term wilderness can be relative – what is a managed agricultural environment to one can be wild and untamed to another. Wales still has a few 'wild' places where you could imagine the imprint of man to be absent, but the trouble with being an ecologist is that you know how much more natural the land could be. For me, conserving arctic-alpine or mountain plants is an attempt to restore some of the essential wildness which is so absent in Britain in the 21st century. The physical and intellectual challenges of how to do this can be daunting, not only is there the whole issue of European and British agricultural policies to deal with, but also the more prosaic matter of getting to the plants. In many of the bigger mountain ranges of the world, access to study mountain plants can be relatively easy. Many grow within metres of the road as in the Alps, or are accessible by téléphérique or just a short walk along a wonderful alpine path. No such advantages in Wales, however. We may have a train to our highest mountain, but that doesn't help if the plants are on any mountain other than Snowdon.

When I first arrived in the Rocky Mountains, I tried not to stand on any *Lloydia* plants, being conditioned into working with its rarity. If you have ever tried to avoid standing on buttercups in a buttercup meadow, you will know how difficult that is. The amusement of the local botanists together with the sheer impossibility of avoiding the 1000's of *Lloydia* plants soon saw me crushing it underfoot with the best of them. We won't ever achieve this abundance in Wales; the environment is not suitable for it to grow in profusion in our mountain grasslands, even if grazing was greatly reduced. It will always be a rock dweller here, but wouldn't it be wonderful if it was abundant enough so that people could see it easily without needing ropes? Or would it? Perhaps we need our rarities? Perhaps we like the feeling that this is something special and to make it more commonplace would destroy its mystique and its attraction ? If we could guarantee that it would remain rare but not decline further, that could be an option, but such rarity can presage extinction, even if it is just a local extinction, so we do need to keep up our conservation efforts, even if it just means running to stand still.

Ravens often accompany me in my work in the Welsh mountains, their throaty cronk piercing the mist while they wheel around keeping an eye on their domain. The collective term for a group of ravens is an Unkindness of ravens. I think that a little harsh for a bird which is more aloof than unkind. The raven is large, robust and at ease in the ruggedness of the Welsh mountains, whereas the Snowdon lily looks delicate and fragile, seemingly completely unsuited to its mountain setting. However, both are superbly adapted to the cold and shaded heights, whilst we struggle to cope with this environment even for a short time.

A botanist friend who died many years ago once said that as mountain botanists in Wales we spend our lives in the shadows, seeking out the hidden gems in the cool, north facing, shaded environment which they favour. We are nowhere near as adapted to this environment as are the Snowdon lily or the raven, but perhaps our intrusions into their world can help to ensure that they continue to enjoy life in the Welsh mountains and that their environment is improved enough to encourage them to increase in numbers and for the plants to spread out of their cliff refuges and continue to delight us for another 10,000 years.

References:
Jones, D. 1996, *The Botanists and Guides of Snowdonia*. Gwasg Carreg Gwalch.
Salisbury, R.A. 1812, *Transactions of the Horticultural Society of London*.

Snowed In

❦

Paula Brackston

My first strong memory of heavy snow comes from the
year I turned thirteen. I was living with my father and
brother near Newtown, in a small cottage near the top
of the high, wind-blown moors that form the Berwyn
mountain range. I say cottage, it was in fact a building
project. A fixer-upper. A couple of small rooms with no
roof. The setting was magical, the view a delight, and the
surrounding countryside glorious.

My father set about putting windows where doors had
been, and doors where windows had been, and constructing
a new roof, and so on. When it was finished it would be
lovely. In the meantime we lived in a caravan with gaslights
and water pumped by generator from a muddy spring at
the bottom of the field. The toilet consisted of a chemical
loo situated in a small stone shed which just happened
to be on the other side of the lane from the caravan. This

didn't matter much, so long as you remembered that on every third Sunday a steady stream of cars filled with Sunday-besters would be passing through to get to the old chapel at the end of the road. That aside, the whole system worked well enough, until winter tightened its icy grip on the place. I knew we were in trouble when I heard ice rattling inside my hot water bottle. To start with we enjoyed the snow, doing all the things teenagers do, such as extreme sledging, vicious snowball fights, and building obscene snowmen, and we were happy. But the snow didn't stop. It kept on and on and on. The caravan wore a fetching white thatch. The water pump froze. The car disappeared into an igloo. We were forced to tunnel to the toilet, and every trip to it required wellies and a warm coat. Not to mention nerves of steel. The memory of the bracing experience of exposing my posterior in sub-zero temperatures with snow falling through the patchy roof remains with me still.

Two years later I was living in the Black Mountains with my mother when another awe-inspiring winter descended. This time the whole village, and indeed the surrounding area for several miles, was isolated for over a week. Feed was dropped by helicopter to starving livestock. The four of us stoked the woodburners and counted ourselves fortunate that my mother had hoarded adequate supplies. Adequate, that is, until a neighbouring family moved in with us. Susan was a single mother with two small children, struggling to cope with a farm even higher up the mountain than ours. Their electricity supply had failed, and they were low on food. We squeezed them into our little cottage, making up beds on sofas and floors. There was a certain excitement about the situation for my brother and I – no school, sport to be had in the snow, helicopters whirring overhead with bales dangling beneath them. However, for my mother it must have been a trial. The neighbour arrived with three hungry mouths, a tin of powdered milk and a bottle of whisky. The whisky barely lasted the weekend. The powdered milk is probably still at the back of a cupboard somewhere. My mother contemplated putting a lock on the fridge door, as Susan was given to nocturnal raids where she would devour half the precious lump of cheddar, or great slices of the boiling bacon that was supposed to feed us all for days to come. And this was not the benign, child-friendly snow I had encountered before. This snow descended at an angle of forty-five degrees and whipped itself around barns and along hedges forming drifts that could swallow you up in a second. The bewildered sheep would huddle against a hedge for shelter only to find themselves quickly buried and unable to get out. Their sheltering places would become tombs if they were not rescued. Exhausting hours were spent pushing sticks into the drifts, searching for the poor ewes, and then digging them out. Despite everyone's frantic efforts, many of them died. The blizzards that swept down the mountain side stung any bare flesh, so that we only dared venture out swaddled in wool to our eyes. The ferocity of the wind was alarming as it wailed and whined around us. It was hard to see and easy to lose your bearings, so that we had to keep shouting to each other to stay safe. That winter I truly learnt to respect the weather on the mountains.

Even so, last February's snow took me by surprise. Our home is one of the few unmodernised longhouses left in Wales. We are situated on the upward rise of the Brecon Beacons, facing back towards the Black Mountains. Our house is thirteen hundred feet up, a mile and a half from our nearest neighbour, and although our views extend for many miles in all directions we cannot see another dwelling.

We have installed a telephone, and we are ridiculously proud of our diesel generator thrumming away in the barn. Otherwise the house is pretty much as it has been for the last six hundred years or so. It is, as you might expect, long and low, and set with its gable end to the prevailing wind, the better to withstand the fearsome gales that assail it frequently through the winter months. We are one small paddock below open mountain, and barely a hundred yards beneath the tree line. They say in the village that it is always two jumpers colder up at our house, and it is true that we appear to have our very own microclimate up here. Us and the mountain. We are a crucial step beyond what most people experience in these parts weather-wise.

We like to think we are prepared. We can't run a freezer due to our part-time power system, but tins and dried pulses and grains keep pretty much indefinitely. It has only ever been the children's need for fresh milk that has sent my partner, Simon, yomping through snow to the village on occasion. Or when he has run out of tobacco, of course. This year we had plenty of warning. The news was full of doom-laden predictions of disruption to travel and heavy falls on high ground. We bought more milk, knowing it would keep well enough on the doorstep in such low temperatures. We stocked up on alcohol. There is something about being besieged, coupled with cold weather, that makes brandy in coffee a must. We purchased extra coal. I got in plenty of tobacco and hid it about the house. We were ready.

The snow, when it came, was of the gentle, beautiful, Perry Como variety. The children (5 and 3) were giddy with glee. They would have been out in it in their pyjamas if I'd let them. I could see why they found it so irresistible. Their muddy world had been transformed under a layer of shamelessly glamorous snow, about six inches deep, fluffy and sparkly and soft. Not a whisper of wind. Perfect for building a snowman or for sledging.

Tad soon found his confidence on the improvised sledge (an old cushion shoved inside a plastic feed sack) and spent happy hours whizzing down a steep incline on his back, his tummy, his bottom, and on one occasion his nose. Nothing dented his enthusiasm. Skyla preferred a chauffeur driven version, clinging to her father as they hurtled down the slope together, sometimes letting go just for the fun of falling off.

It was well worth the fifteen minutes it took to find the right foot for the right welly, jam hats onto heads, push tiny hands into thermal mittens, and cover them in waterproof clothing. It was even worth the grizzling as cold penetrated to their fingers, and the whinging when they were dragged back inside. They sat by the fire, faces aglow, eyes bright, munching warm pancakes as their ears tingled on in the afterglow of their snowy activities.

On the second day, we had expected a bit of a thaw. Instead we woke to flakes the size of hamsters falling silently onto the already white landscape. It snowed and snowed and snowed. For seven hours. By mid afternoon there was over a foot of snow. Every twig on every branch of every tree was coated in ermine. Anything with leaves was forced to bow low beneath the weight of the frozen water.

Simon took Tad off for a boys' walk, sneaking out while Skyla napped.

When she woke up she was furious at being thought of as too young and persuaded me to take her out. Just a short shuffle, I thought. Skyla had other ideas. Despite the fact that the snow was, at the very least, over her knees, she wanted to explore. And who could blame her? There was an otherworldly quality to the stillness and silence that surrounded us. All colour had vanished, leaving the scenery monochrome.

We crossed a stream with snow to its very edges and stepping-stones wearing snow as tall as chefs' hats. Skyla reached up with a stick and rattled the branches of a hazel tree, creating her own little snowstorm. She flopped into drifts, lying on her back to stare up at the sock-grey sky still full of snow. She shook snow from a stooped bough of holly only to see it ping up to ten feet above her head when she let it go. She found tracks of birds and rabbits and hares and mice. I watched her, letting myself experience the beauty and mystery of the place through her fascinated eyes, as if for the first time.

It took us an hour to do a short walk we would ordinarily have completed in fifteen minutes. I had to drag and manhandle her the last stage of the outing as we crossed a field where the snow lay so thick it was above her waist. She didn't utter a word of complaint – she was so enthralled by her surroundings.

That evening, with the small ones sleeping soundly – no doubt dreaming of huskies and '*Narnia*' and '*Christmas, The Sequel*' – we adults slumped on sofas sipping a warming Shiraz. A sudden rumbling noise had us all rushing to the window. A low flying jet? The generator exploding?

The sound was a giant's roar in the snow-muted sounds we had become accustomed to. A clearing sky allowed the waxing moon to illuminate the cause of the noise. The roof of the barn on the far side of our yard had collapsed under the weight of the snow.

It says something about modern building standards that the two older barns (one probably fifteenth century, the other built in the early eighteen hundreds) were still standing, icy but undamaged. The nineteen sixties breezeblock construction, by contrast, was now a tangle of beams and asbestos sheeting. Having an inadequate pitch, the A-frames had been unable to stand the pressure exerted by the snow and had imploded beneath it. It was hard to believe that those gentle, noiseless flakes could hold such destructive power.

Beneath the mangled remains of the barn lay our vintage caravan, now sporting the unusual feature of oak beams. Our beloved pick-up truck was trapped but miraculously escaped with only minor cuts and bruises. The following morning the thaw began, a dripping, slippery, grey-muddy mess of an event. Within a matter of hours the snow had gone. What remained was the fractured and tangled skeleton of the barn, an ugly monument to the force of nature.

When the ground dries up we will knock it down and soon grass will grow over the scarred earth and the view will be all the better for the barn's absence. What will endure far longer, however, are the images imprinted on my mind from those two days of whiteness, when the mountain slumbered beneath a duvet of snow, and my children's faces shone in the light reflected off the glittering surface of the land.

Alternative Boots

❦

Katherine Cuthbert

Once I had taken access to the Welsh hills and countryside for granted. I had been brought up in Aberystwyth in the nineteen fifties and early sixties. My parents were enthusiastic walkers and so, with my two sisters, I was introduced to this activity at an early age. Initially we joined in walks in the countryside immediately around the town – Penglais and Cwm woods, along the Rheidol river, and over the cliff path. After the acquisition of the family car, we were able to get further afield. I still remember the excitement of my first climb up a proper mountain – Cadair Idris – those huge dark cliffs above Llyn Cau, and the tremendous views from the top made a great impression on me.

By the early nineteen seventies I was married and living

over the border. Our outdoor life included cycling and skiing as well as walking. Active outings were an important part of weekend relaxation. They provided a vital source of renewal after we had been working inside all week. We spent our summer holidays walking, or cycle touring in this country or on the continent.

Then, in the summer of 1993 my life, and to a lesser extent that of my partner, changed completely. We were towards the end of a cycling holiday in Bavaria when my left leg started to give way. As I climbed the stairs to our hotel bedroom, I found that my legs felt amazingly heavy. Within a month I had received a diagnosis of multiple sclerosis.

It was a huge shock to go so quickly from being apparently fit and healthy to having a severe chronic illness and considerable walking difficulties. As is usual with MS there have been ups and downs in my condition and capabilities. Now things seem to have steadied out. I can walk, but not far. My legs get very tired, very quickly. At best I can just about manage a mile, but that is pretty much it – my legs are near to collapse.

By the summer of 1996 I came to the reluctant conclusion that I needed to acquire a wheelchair. The positive intention was that it would enable me to go to places and do things that wouldn't otherwise be possible. I was going to be using the chair on my own terms. I would be a part-time wheelchair user.

I was kind of pleased with my acquisition. It did, as I had hoped, improve my countryside mobility – at least to a degree. It enabled me to get back to visiting local countryside parks where paths are generally quite well surfaced. I soon adopted a strategy of walking a bit while pushing the chair, and then riding and self-propelling when I got tired. I wasn't too keen on being pushed. But wheeling by pushing the wheel hand rims is hard work and getting over rough or uneven ground in my conventional manual wheelchair was pretty much impossible for me. I wanted more than this.

But then I had a lucky break, and new and greater opportunities emerged. This was as a result of finding out about handcycles. What on earth is a *hand*cycle you might ask? My handcycle is my wheelchair with another wheel fitted in front. This third wheel has an up-tube which allows for the attachment of chain wheels, 21 speed derrailleur gears and handlebars.

Suddenly, the wheelchair becomes a completely different kind of machine. Now, I can crank the handlebars in a circular movement, rather than having to strain on the wheel rims. This is a great deal easier. The gears mean that I can change down a gear when I come to an incline and there is at least some chance of getting up lesser hills. I don't want to give the wrong impression. Using a handcycle is still quite hard work – especially for a middle aged woman not endowed with well-developed biceps!

Even so, it has very many advantages over a conventional manual wheelchair if you want to get out into real countryside. Since we acquired the handcycle in 1998 we have explored quite a few possibilities. Some of these, inevitably, represent paths that are more accessible such as forestry routes, old railway trails, and canal side paths. But with a little bit of effort more interesting and exciting routes can still be found. There are plenty of these in various parts of Wales.

In the days before MS we had explored parts of the Pembrokeshire Coast Path. Now there are greater problems. Narrow paths and quite strenuous ascents and descents do not make for good, or even possible handcycling. But we have found that there are quite a number of sections of the path that continue to be accessible. One which has now become a springtime favourite for us is Newport and the Nevern estuary towards the northern end of the National Park.

The Parrog is the old port area of Newport, dating from the 1700s and before. There is a convenient car park next to the Boat Club which is an old stone building that had once been a harbour warehouse. There are a couple of ruined lime kilns facing onto the quayside, and there is a cottage which was apparently once the Newport mortuary. As with so many of the Pembrokeshire coastal villages you still get a sense of the port that used to be.

Just along from the car park the road descends to the beach and the path becomes what is almost a narrow causeway, especially when the tide is in. There is just about space for my handcycle! In the spring sea pinks seem to grow out of almost every cranny in the old stone walls.

Beyond the causeway, old Parrog cottages with stonewalled front gardens are lined up closely together along the harbour-side wall. House martins continually fly in and out of nests under the eaves of one of the houses. A few sailing boats are beached on the mud below. This mud is actually reasonably firm. A narrow lane opens directly onto the estuary-side just past the cottages and the shore side is often the most convenient place for turning a car around. The low rounded rocks humping out of the sand, with associated green fringed pools, need to be avoided by cars, but provide attractions for exploring children.

A short diversion along the stony and rocky foreshore (when the tide is out) brings one to the proper road in front of the much grander, much larger houses which once belonged to merchants and sea captains. Soon the road climbs very gently and becomes an accessible path. Now we are above low cliffs and then a small sandy cove. At low tide the river Nevern curves in closely under these cliffs. An old, disused lifeboat station sits just above the cove. It was badly placed because the estuary sand bar extends quite far over and makes launching difficult at certain states of the tide.

Although I don't usually associate them with the seaside the most prominent birds here are swallows which sweep and soar endlessly, seemingly appreciating this space above the sea. There are other birds on the shore below. Piercing cries alert us to the presence of oyster catchers scrabbling in the seaweed among the rocks. Their black and white plumage, orange beaks and pink legs draw our visual attention.

As well as this close entertainment we have marvellous

longer views. Up the estuary Carn Ingli, that imposing outlier of the Preseli hills stands out and, across this estuary in miniature, there is the broad expanse of Newport Sands with sand dunes behind.

Yet further along on the Parrog side the path becomes a cliff side route. If I want to go on I have to abandon the handcycle. There is a tricky (for me) but very short stretch of steep rocky path. It has been worn quite smooth by the passage of many feet. There is a very big step and nothing to hold on to. In the narrow space it is impossible for anybody else to help. Keeping secure and keeping my balance is difficult. I almost feel that I am a climber. I really have to be very careful about where I place my feet. But I do want to get further so I take the risk.

Once I have overcome this challenge the cliff path becomes easier. Slowly, and with care, I can walk here. Our target is to achieve the grassy spot that allows us to look straight down the steep cliff face to the kind of rocky cove which typifies the coastal path. In the spring we expect to find patches of the lovely sky blue, star-like squill flowers. These flowers are quite small, but a mass of them has a strong presence. There are more sea pinks or thrift flowers here, often in varying degrees of pinkness. There are also white sea campions, the flowers we used to make into skirted 'ladies' as children. If we are lucky we might see some yellow kidney vetch with rather clumpy flowers, like small pom-poms, probably positioned part way down the cliff.

This is a good spot for a rest. But if we take the return

path to the car park we can then take a very different route in the opposite direction. This is a broad, easy and predominantly flat path directly alongside the higher reaches of the estuary. I am free to handcycle fast and leave my companions behind if I wish. At high tide the water will be glimmering through the bordering trees. At low tide there is grey mud on either side of the narrow channel of the river. In spring, the new leaves on the trees can almost turn the track into a green tunnel.

We soon reach the white-painted iron bridge over the now narrowed estuary. At the right state of the tide there is likely to be a statuesque heron standing tall over a muddy pool. When potential prey is seen the neck is stretched forward and then, as appropriate, there is a sudden jabbing down.

Across the bridge, the estuary-side path is a great deal narrower and uneven. But it is still reasonably flat, and with care, I can continue to handcycle. It is probably a good precaution to put some gloves on, even in summer. The backs of hands are exposed when you handcycle and stings, from overhanging nettles are an annoying irritation.

A mile or so on the path turns to the right and we cross the dune based golf course. Then, we are soon down on the beach at Newport Sands. Sandy beaches are, by their nature, flat, wide and open and have a wonderfully spacious feel. Pembrokeshire beaches, with views of sea, dramatic cliffs and green headlands provide exhilarating handcycling. At Newport beach there is now a very attractive view back across the estuary to the cottages and larger houses alongside which we had previously been walking. We are now able to see beyond to the previously hidden, distinctively shaped Dinas Head beyond Fishguard Bay. By the time we get back to the car park on the other side of the estuary I feel that I have had a good day's handcycling through some wonderfully varied landscapes.

Using the handcycle means that I am able to get to all sorts of places which would otherwise be impossible. I feel that I can get *into* the countryside. I am not bounded by roads and tarmac. I have a sense of freedom and opportunity.

On some of our outings we no longer get very far. I think that I have a different attitude to distance these days. A short handcycle ride in an especially beautiful spot is to be fully savoured. We sit, rest and enjoy the beauty of where we are more thoroughly than we might once have done. Then we would have been impatient to get on. Now we feel a greater freedom to linger and appreciate.

But when conditions and terrain are right it *is* possible to get much further. There are quite a few paths where I can enjoy handcycling for seven or eight miles. Also, there are places where, with a degree of effort, it is possible to find accessible mountain paths. The feeling of being actively out in the great outdoors is very important. I may have to work quite hard. I get out of breath. My arms get tired. But this physical exertion is all part of the experience and the achievement.

Of course, it is now more difficult to find good routes.

Maps no longer tell us all the things we need to know. Promising paths can become too narrow, or impossibly rocky and uneven. Quite often we find ourselves facing a stile or kissing gate. These are obviously no problem for the able-bodied walker, but if you are a disabled handcyclist they are a serious and frustrating impediment. Because of these problems route finding becomes a greater challenge.

Now finding a new path that is accessible, but also takes us to and through beautiful places is cause for celebration. There is a sense of accomplishment – even triumph. My handcycle gives me these feelings of freedom. I can no longer walk very far, but I can still get out and enjoy the peace and impressiveness of the Welsh landscape.

Y Coity

❦

Martha Stephens

The Coity Mountain is part of the post-industrial landscape of Torfaen, not picture postcard Wales – a plumper, plainer sister to nearby Sugar Loaf, but a mountain of more substance. A stately old lady. Most of this mountain's slopes and curves have been defaced. It has been scarred with quarries and pockmarked with mines, but it retains its dignity.

On a clear day, the panorama from the broad top plateau is spectacular, but I don't climb the steep sides for the views. I have a more intimate relationship with this mountain. I find pleasure in the detail. The violent weather. The rhythm of my stride along skinny, sheep-worn paths. The whistling whisper of the wind in the heather. The earthy fragrance after a rain shower and the sharpness of an under-ripe whinberry on my tongue. The journey to the top is never just a race to ponder the horizon.

In autumn the predominant colours of the mountain are russets and rusts. The long dying grass stalks are shades of ochre. They are bent double and snap beneath my feet. Dewy early morning walks soak my trousers to the knees. The huge dragon's head of bracken, which lies on the north-eastern bank, loses its summer camouflage and becomes bold and red again. After a night of heavy drenching rain I have to leap swollen ditches, my feet disappearing into sodden, soft, black peat banks.

In winter the wind is so strong that as I reach the crest of the mountain it takes my breath away. The windy days make me silly. I giggle and skip as I'm nudged and buffeted across the plateau. Some days the rain is relentless and horizontal. The mountain tests my resolve. I have to tear myself from my fire and push myself up the steep slope. I walk until the icy rain seeps through layers of clothes to my skin. It always finds a way in – seams or cuffs, under storm flaps and through zips. On the first shiver I turn downwards for the valley. Once home and dry I experience a weary elation. Glad that I pushed myself to make the climb.

On freezing days the northern slope, scarcely glanced upon by the sun, wears its crisp white frosting for days. Deep drifts and pockets of snow remain for weeks.

In spring I can climb in clear sunshine and descend in soaking rain. Some mornings, dense grey cloud sits on top like a new hairdo. A strand of mist coils and drifts down the slopes like an escaping curl. A myriad of peculiar, brightly coloured fungi, algae and lichen decorate the rocks and screes. Fat streams, fed by the winter thaw, burst from between rocks and crash and tumble down their courses to the valley bottom.

In late summer, the mountain is at its best. It is blanketed with a patchwork of purple heather and vivid green whinberry shrubs. The bracken is waist-high and where flattened, offers sheltered private places to rest. I climb in the cool of the evenings to reach the top before the sun sets. I lie on the springy heather and watch the stars appear, one at a time, then couples, then constellations. Being above the sodium glows of Blaenavon and Brynmawr, I see milky swathes of stars that are invisible from my garden. Lying under the vast sky I am put in my place. I am reminded of my insignificance. My past and future are put into perspective. My presence in this world will be too brief to register in the history of the mountain.

Whatever the time of year, I can be caught out by sudden changes in the weather. A thick fog can roll in from nowhere and swallow the mountain in seconds. Landmarks vanish and with them my bearings. Old Lady Coity becomes sulky, resentful, she wants her privacy. Then, the mountain is suddenly frightening. I become disorientated, slightly panicked. Several times I have been lost for hours in the fog. Lost, then stumbling, then plunging thigh-deep into peaty, water-filled troughs. On these occasions I seek out a place to wait, a fleece-flecked hole carved by generations of sheep seeking shelter. I wait for a break in the fog, a fleeting window that allows me to escape the summit and make my way down, relieved that I hadn't stepped into a shaft, or over the crumbling edge of a quarry.

The mountain is littered with pits and mines and quarries and heaps of rain-sculpted slag. They are remnants of the dirty trades on which the local towns were built. There is a working coal mine on one of the planes. It is an obscene grubby reminder of this mountain's vulnerability. There is still coal here and this mountain is still being exploited.

The most treasured aspect of my relationship with this mountain is the complete and utter solitude. You can't park on the top in a crowded car park and jostle for a glance at the view, as on the nearby Blorenge. Nobody walks here. I have scattered startled sheep, been appraised by wary mountain ponies, been swooped upon by protective buzzard parents with young nestled in the nooks and crannies of an abandoned quarry. Dozens of small birds bob and skim over the heather, but I have never encountered another human being while walking the Coity.

This mountain helps me grow and now reflects parts of me. Old Lady Coity is scarred; damaged, but resilient. She is not pretty but she has majesty. I watch her soften the quarries and heal the wounds of the old workings. She gradually, inch by inch, reclaims the sooty heaps of spoil. Lakes and ponds lie scattered about, like shiny coins spilled from her purse, where there were once filthy pits. She forgives but she doesn't forget. While exploring her plump contours I have met her challenges and discovered my inner strengths. When I lie in her purple heather skirts I find her secrets, enjoy her gifts, and experience true wonder, deep peace and simple contentment.

Leaving Pencaer

✿

Gwyneth Evans

*'Pencaer, cerrig llwydon – lle drwg I fagu da,
lle da I fagu lladfron!'*

*'Pencaer of the grey rocks – bad place for rearing
cattle, a good place to breed bandits!'*

It would be a strange feeling, saying 'Goodbye' to Nia, a
feeling I would be unable to explain to anyone else, because
Nia existed only in my thoughts. There, she was often my
heroine, my guide, and even at times, my spiritual comfort.
Now the time had come, I would need her no longer…

It was 1984. My father had just told me that he was
giving up the tenancy of our farm situated on Pencaer,
that unique headland in North Pembrokeshire, where our

farm nestled among notable landmarks such as Carreg Gwastad, the landing place of the French invaders in 1797, and Strumble Head lighthouse. It is a rough, rock strewn landscape, haunted by the ghosts of legendary Celtic giants, surrounded on three sides by the Atlantic seas, full of stories of seals, shipwrecks and mermaids.

My father and I, and his father before him, had farmed this piece of Pencaer for a total of 55 years. In that time there had been many changes in farming practice. It seemed that the pace of change was accelerating. We could no longer keep up.

Some years before, a neighbour had shown me what he claimed was a flint axe head that he had found while walking across his ploughed field. 'It's a stone,' I said, looking at it where it lay in his not too clean hand. 'It's an axe head,' he insisted, 'Look!' I looked but was not convinced. It was just a stone to me. I imagined that I must have seen hundreds like it on my walks around Pencaer and not realised they were of any significance. A few days later, my neighbour rang to say that a man from the Museum had confirmed it was indeed a flint tool from the Iron Age. 'He wants to see you,' said my neighbour, 'Can I send him over?' I was surprised, I was sure that I did not have much in the way of knowledge to share with someone so learned. (After all, I didn't know my Neolithic from my Palaeolithic, and still don't.) Nevertheless I welcomed him into the house.

My mother, in her usual manner of dealing with anyone in authority, escaped to feed the calves, preferring the company of the animals to that of our visitor. He soon told me what he wanted. He had heard that on nearby land were some strange humps and mounds and thought that I could show him where they were. I was delighted as I had played on the mounds as a child, and often wondered what had caused them.

We trudged along muddy pathways, heads bent against the force of the wind, towards the moor. My dog, Carlo, led the way, delighted with this break from his usual routine. At the site of the strange mounds, the Museum Man scrambled onto the hedge to get a better view of the humps and bumps. 'Please, be careful,' I shouted trying to get him to hear me above the noise of the wind. 'Those stones are loose and slippery.' He took no notice of the warning, and jumped off the hedge down to the other side. There he waved his arms about, his finger pointing at the ground all around him. 'Iceni!' He shouted back, 'They came west into Wales after Boadicea was defeated by the Romans! This looks like a typical settlement, and quite a big one.' He pointed again, 'Look! You can see the boundaries go a lot further, right into the next couple of fields.'

He climbed back onto the hedge. 'So they're hut circles?' I asked. He nodded, and bounced down off the hedge. 'Yes, they're very interesting,' he pointed again. 'What a pity it has been so destroyed! You can tell what has happened,' his arm swept around to the view beyond the site. 'Over the centuries the stones have been removed to build all these.' He indicated the Independent Chapel, with its Vestry, and adjoining caretaker's house. The nearby farm buildings, cottages and the patchwork of small fields surrounded by stone walls. As we returned to the farmyard, now with our backs to the wind, he told me a little of what he knew about the Iceni.

I was intrigued when he told me that it was possible that they had taken over an even earlier settlement, possibly from the Iron Age, as I knew there were the remains of Iron Age fortifications on nearby Garn Fawr. What was more fascinating to me was the thought that a follower of Boadicea, perhaps a strong, brave, warrior-type of female had lived in this place, 2000 years before me, and I was now walking in her footsteps, perhaps doing the same kind of things she had done. Like me, she may have had to do battle with the elements on Pencaer's weather worn hills, to tend to her animals. 'The Iceni,' he informed me, 'used oxen to plough the land, sometimes as many as six at a time.'

Not here, I thought, looking at my feet where the land was peppered with stones, but I was still intrigued by the thought of my 2000 year old counterpart. Over the next few days, with the help of a book from the local library, I read a bit more about the Iceni. I could imagine how hard her daily life must have been. I decided 'she' had to have a name, so I called her Nia – it gave her a kind of reality. She was no longer merely a figure from history.

Then, if my cold fingers got jammed in a gate, or the rain from the sea turned to snow, blocking the narrow roads, or when one of our animals became lame, or the sly fox carried away yet another newborn lamb, I would think of Nia, and wonder how she might have coped with the same situation 2000 years before. Would she have cried, or muttered a few rude words, or shrugged her shoulders and carried on? In the summer months Pencaer was a different place to what it was in the harsher months of the winter. Summer visitors delighted in telling us how lucky we were to live in such a beautiful place. They were there in July or August, when the breeze from the sea was refreshing, the grass was green and the heat from the summer sun would be ripening the growing corn, making the air shimmer in the heat. On a summer evening, away to the west the sun would be setting. A flame-red ball, gradually extinguished by the Atlantic waves rolling in to Abermawr. Then a spark of light would flash far out to sea; the beam from the lighthouse on the North Bishop Rock. As dusk turned to darkness, the haunting cry of the curlew and the croak of a raven heading back to its nest on Pwllderi's cliffs, would lull you to sleep.

From September to April, it seemed that we waged a constant battle against the elements. Farmers are notorious for moaning about the weather and we were no different. Pencaer, during the winter months, was a challenge. We would argue amongst ourselves over the simplest of tasks, such as whose turn it was to fetch in the cows for milking. After a day of wind and rain, your clothes would already have had a couple of soakings, so putting them on again was punishment.

Even Carlo would look at you in disgust as you called him out from the shelter of the barn. The wind, coming from the direction of Abermawr would be 'veering south westerly, gale force 8' according to the shipping forecast, but it felt more like a hurricane, especially when there was only one tree between you and Ireland. The cows, huddled together in the lee of a hawthorn hedge would pointedly ignore your calls to come and be milked. Then, when you sent Carlo to chivvy them, they would suddenly decide to move, and almost trample over you in the narrow gateways, in their haste to get to the relative shelter of the cattle yards. By now the driven rain would have found its way, cold and merciless, down inside the collar of your so called 'waterproofs'.

True happiness may not arrive with the latest fashions or a shiny new car, but a nice warm kitchen and a blazing fire on a cold wet day must come close. Poor Nia, she must have spent a large part of her day looking for fuel and keeping a fire going. What if I was spirited back to 2000 years ago? What would I be faced with? No telephones, televisions, milking machines, no car, so what did I have to moan about? I would ask myself this question as I trudged after a recalcitrant cow through a sea of mud. While Nia may have had her own difficulties, she had one advantage over the modern farmer – not for her the endless form filling and Income Tax, PAYE and VAT returns!

My twenty years of farming saw many changes. To say that mechanisation saved work is something of a fallacy. What it allowed you to do was a lot more work in the same amount of time. Owning expensive equipment meant you had to spend time servicing it, so that it was maintained at peak efficiency. Where Nia would have spent some minutes sharpening her axe, I had to do battle with engines, bulk tanks and pipeline milking systems. My mother never minded scalding out the milk buckets, she had done so for years, and the introduction of stainless steel had made the job a lot easier. The modern pipeline system stretched her capabilities, and as for washing the system out after each twice-daily milking, well, she just never got the hang of it. There were so many flow taps to be changed to divert different liquids in various directions. She would turn the wrong taps, and we would hear a scream, and then the electric motor cutting out. In a panic she would have pushed the red emergency stop button, because she could see detergent and water heading towards the tank, full of creamy, clean, fresh milk! It should have been heading out of harm's way into the drains. That button helped avoid many a disaster.

Artificial fertilisers also came into popular usage in my time on the farm. The first field of hay that we used a baler in yielded 250 bales. A couple of years later, with the addition of nitrogen, the same field yielded 900 bales. The production of more food for the animals meant you could increase your herd, creating – a lot more work.

As the years passed, so our farm evolved from the traditional mixed family farm, which was the usual in the late fifties and early sixties, to a beef cattle and dairy enterprise. Gone were the horses, the chickens, hens, ducks, pigs and sheep, now all unprofitable unless farmed by a more intensive method. As farming methods changed and machinery replaced hand work, so farming neighbours became independent, and we saw less of them. The sense of close community cooperation was diminished. Quite often during those years I thought of my imaginary friend, and in a way she kept me company as I worked. After 45 years of farming my father decided he'd had enough, and in June 1985, we sold the large part of our dairy herd. In the autumn we put a deposit on our new home in the town of Fishguard, not very far away, and it seemed only natural to name the house 'Pencaer'.

In October 1985, after we had held the clear out sale of all our stock, crops and farming implements, we could then plan our move from old Pencaer. I was not sad, I knew the spirit of Nia was still there in that place, still in those grey rocks, the soil and the air. Yes, she would be staying on, and keeping a close eye on it for me.

Skomer Log

❦

Jane Matthews

Drizzle is increasing as I sit on the cliff-top at Amy's Reach. A buzzard calls in alarm above me, the sea licks at the beach below and a fat, moulting pup looks up with a puzzled look, surely uncomfortable in its bloated, immobile state. I think back: my most profound memory at this point is leaving the M4 at Junction 5 – Langley, Slough, just west of Heathrow, en route to a construction company where I spend three weeks carving a 20ft polystyrene nose through which a B-list celebrity will emerge in the name of Comic Relief. My life as a Scenic Artist in the television and film industry is as bizarre and ridiculous as the fictitious worlds I help create; secret worlds where cosy interiors are pinned together in warehouse studios, I have succeeded in my job if nothing is what it seems.

Now on Skomer I exist in an equally unusual world, but this is a very real, raw, primal place where I feel mist on my face, earth on my hands and live in tune with the natural world. I relish this contrast but will never return to Langley.

Our house stands proud over the sea at North Haven, surrounded at the various stages of the summer by lush carpets of bluebells or red campion, and crowds of puffins. These mad little seabird characters share our panoramic view from their hillside burrows; of sea, sky, and the St. David's Peninsula to the north. Lining the banks they spill off like petals, a giant swathe of cascading birds that precedes us as we cross the narrow path from the landing point. In small groups they are more plucky, twitching as we approach, but valiantly dare-devil, holding out until we are upon them, until one gives in and they all take flight; paddles pointed, wings fluttering, beaks down.

The Warden's house has nestled on this cliff top amongst the puffins for over fifty years, with gas lights, a wood burner and intermittent power from a few car batteries and a solar panel. It is made of wood and bellows in a gale but keeps us (and scores of scrabbling mice) dry in the fiercest storms. Throughout the summer it creaks and sighs in the midday heat and reminds me of what a treat it is to live here in such a wild little wonderland. Mine has been a bizarre journey from voluntary warden (a weekly scheme that sounded like a perfect break from London's mayhem), to one month as a lazy lovebird, receiving novels and chocolate in parcels from my friends and watching the sun sparkle across the water and rabbits hop out of the bracken to feed on the grass at my feet, to the day when I decide that London is best avoided and Skomer would be a fine place to live a little, with my new partner, its warden.

This small off-shore National Nature Reserve hosts a dazzling festival of creation that becomes more arresting with each year I spend here. Skomer is a breeding ground for millions of seabirds that return to land each year for the busy summer months. With over 6000 pairs of puffins, 20,000 guillemots, 6000 razorbills and up to 125,000 thousand pairs of Manx shearwaters there is no quiet moment between March and September.

Nights are filled with the cries of the Manx shearwaters that dart, swoop and crash out of the velvet darkness on their return to their burrows from the sea. It is a unique sound; indescribably emotive, eerie yet upbeat and wilful, a laughing, cooing cry. One pair lives under the house and starts up their noisy reunion, one from its shift at sea to the other incubating a creamy white egg below the floorboards.

As summer advances and most of the seabird species leave, the resident grey seals start to nose around the shores, big swollen females looking for their ideal spot to play out their yearly breeding ritual. Autumn then gets its accompaniment of calling pups, sing-howling adults and angry bulls.

I spend four months each year studying this breeding seal population. The job involves daily detailed observations of seal activity; births, deaths and marriages. Each pup receives a coloured spray-mark from me on the base of its back – a temporary code that enables it to be tracked for its first three weeks of life until the pup moults its white coat and gains independence from its mother. This is the closest I get to a vocational crossover – a throwback to my days as a scenic artist, but on this incredible natural stage.

I identify seals that return to the same section of a beach at the same time of year – in some cases to the day – to give birth. I watch for hours as a labouring cow shifts in the shingle, knowing but nonchalant, an undisturbed birth of breathtaking simplicity that concludes like clockwork with two noses exchanging scent. The pleasure sparkles through me. By this point I am four months away from my own labour and Skomer is to have its youngest human inhabitant for years.

Each day throughout the autumn I trek out to the main beaches at which the seals haul out and sleep at low tide. I fall into line, dictated to by the moon and its pull on the water and my weeks are staggered by the daily shifts in tides. I relish this pattern and as I sit beneath greying skies, counting the mosaic of twitching bodies below, I wonder if this is wearing off on the unborn I carry with me; an instinct, an affinity, sea, tides, moon, the daily patterns of this nature that I have the pleasure of looking in on. I start a diary in the hope that I can capture some of this treasure for her.

We return to Skomer after three months over-wintering on the mainland, two weeks after giving birth to our daughter. I feel like I have been hit by a bus. Despite vowing to adopt the seal's approach I fail miserably and miss out on any of the earth-mother euphoria that I planned for. On a remote island in March with little heating and no mains electricity, few luxuries and no grandmothers on hand I feel slightly bewildered. Life becomes a long line of cold tea, mugs left just out of reach as I sit for the majority of the day feeding Skomer's newest addition. Between feeds on fine days I scrub laundry in the bath and pass it through a mangle.

5th May 2005

This afternoon you lay in the beanbag on the grass outside the house beneath sheets that clapped and billowed on the line above; you were mesmerised by the moving shapes against the spring blue sky – what perfect entertainment. The bluebells are just beginning to flower and it feels like summer is on its way at last; happy days, even though I haven't had a proper night's sleep for months.

The following week I venture ashore for the first time as a mother, park the car and forget to engage the handbrake. No one gets hurt and it's nothing the insurance won't cover but I realise Skomer's advantages. No cars, no shops, no closing times; I live a strange existence free from the usual tags and routines that punctuate daily life. Weather fronts and the sea state dictate our movements, our visitors and our chances of fresh food. If it rains we stay indoors, if it is fine we spend all day outside. As autumn approaches again I start to re-synchronise with the tides, the seals begin to pup and I take my daughter to see all she experienced last year from within.

We bridge a momentous gap that signals great changes to the island's superstructure – renovations, new buildings and technologies that promise to bring our living into the Twenty-first Century. From the very basic, where water is boiled for drinking, lights are lit by hand and a few spare volts of power are a bonus, we look towards double glazing, power sockets and pure water. Our beautifully characterful (but aged) house is flattened and we reside temporarily in what is essentially a shed with a hole in the roof, no shower, no bath and only an outside toilet 50 metres away. Autumn sounds like it is trying to break-and-enter through our door but the island's beauty keeps me from domestic gloom.

27ᵗʰ October 2005

Now that the storm has passed the sky is bright and pale, long purple shadows stretch over the dying bracken – a rich russet orange. Autumn will be fine as long as we don't run out of food, but the field mushrooms and rabbits can keep us going for a while yet. Today's wind is warm, the warmest October day in London for over a hundred years apparently, according to Radio 4. Here it's warmer than cold. They say we are due for orange rain tomorrow, coming up from the Sahara laden with sand.

The seal rounds are complete and you are now asleep on my back, heavy and quiet and enjoying the ride. Some days pass with no real focus, none needed, and this I quite like. Today is full of beautiful colour and passing birds, nothing more. The wood sage shivers in the wind and the generator hums like a ferry.

A year later the new house is unfurling at North Haven, so sheepish and slow that the puffins hardly notice. We get alternative (less primitive) accommodation in the meantime, gradually increasing the doses of technology and convenience so that by the time we move into our new home we will think nothing of flicking on a laptop or reading after nightfall under stark electric lights.

23rd October 2006

A day of beautiful washed sunshine, buffeting wind and rough, frothing sea. The rushing swell fills every cranny of the rocks before falling like streamers. Foam blows up like snow and catches on the headland amid the rich mustard lichen. Moo-ing cows deter the advancing bull on the beach below, sending him back ceremoniously to the water. You will be waiting at home for me when I return – too heavy

to carry out with me now. Squealing when you see me at
the door you will come running – pink sandals on red vinyl,
dap, dap, dap… 'ellowww'.

The views over the island's central fields are staggering;
linear and bright, streaked with purples and pinks
throughout the summer, pallid with fog caught in the
skeletal bracken on the bleakest days in autumn. After a
year and a half in accommodation in the centre of the island
it is a thrill to be back again at North Haven in our new
home. The familiar sounds of gulls echoing round the bay
and the labouring engine of the Dale Princess offloading
its visitors punctuate the summer. Puffins, butterflies, long
grass, dusty tracks, cold shallows and happy days. A world
away from the M4.

October is deliciously warm, bugs hum in the banks as
I take to the cliff paths again, my last season with Skomer
and its seals. My daughter is now alongside, jumping
the burrows in the paths in her bright red duffle coat,
chattering about pebbles, flowers and taking the big boat
to Shetland. Gossamer threads float over the cliff top
and chough pierce the crisp air with their distinctive call.
Dark, stark shadows cut across the bracken and we watch
a prowling bull seal in the water below, a dark shifting
shadow himself loitering with intent. Freshly marked
pups splash in the iridescent shallows, one corkscrewing
through the water, nosing its mother and then riding on
her back. Nostalgia will start to creep in as the adventure

shifts to a new beginning – easier and yet harder in so many ways. However, Skomer remains unique, spectacular and magical, and our lives there equally so. Nothing can ever be quite the same.

Seeking the Positives

※

Ruth Joseph

It had been a tough year. My previously contented situation seemed irretrievable for work finished abruptly with a heated discussion over a difference of principles, while in my private life I was still smarting from the hurt of a friend's careless words that left our decades-old friendship damaged beyond repair. I'd never coped or welcomed arguments, labelled 'the sensitive one'. Now my agonies continued, persistent, unrelenting. I kept telling myself that there were those who had so much less than I and survived, I had my wonderful family, other good friends. I watched a child in the park near where I lived managing in a wheelchair.

Look at her I told myself, *she's laughing, she's coping. It's about time you dealt with the matter and binned the angst. Count your blessings and get on with your life.*

Easier said than done.

I reminded myself that my grandchildren would be coming for tea. In a few minutes I'd be cuddling two tiny children clothed in miniature jeans and dainty pink tops embroidered with fairies and puppies who gave me wet kisses and tight hugs, wrote me cards adorned with stick-on hearts and glitter and adored my cooking. I'd watch them as they sat sipping my homemade pea soup, eating boiled eggs with soldiers, my whimberry crumble and custard, with ribboned golden curls bobbing tight in bunches and bright blue eyes like scraps of sky, full of ready giggles and tears. We'd play Magic Fishing, Happy Families and riotous games of Snakes and Ladders. I'd read to them about Hairy Maclary of Donaldson's Dairy. They were my precious babies. Then they would go home and the house would return to its previous sounds of television, the News and Match of the Day.

After they had gone and supper finished we went to bed, both tired.

'They were lovely weren't they?'

'Yes,' he yawned, 'wonderful, it's late. I'm shattered. Go to sleep.'

I tried to sleep but my bed usually comfortable had transformed itself into another place to agonise. He breathed with a soft snore next to me and I turned and watched the silhouette of his shoulder through the gloom of the bedroom lit by the streetlight outside. Eventually I slept a fitful sleep jangling with nightmares, waking to images that pained my consciousness.

Each day remained the same. Waking to a routine of

hurt. Acute, unmanageable. I walked in the park and gazed at the vast camellia bushes looking for the earliest bud and that flower's tentative opening. In the past I celebrated the first camellia as if it was a personal birthday. It was my symbol that winter was past. Then I'd look for snowdrops emerging out of the frozen ground and rejoice in the sight of one small white flower nodding in a still icy breeze. And I'd know that spring was mine to enjoy. But this year the pain stayed with me as agonising as the first moment of wounding.

We decided to spend a few days in North Wales.

'We'll stay in a friendly B and B, walk by the sea in Criccieth. Have lunch in a café. Hunt through a few antique shops, eh?' he said.

And I nodded thinking a change of landscape would be good. But as we drove with the radio fixed on the classical station, villages and towns slipping past, through the winter backdrop and the Brecon Beacons, bleak in a misty fog with knots of sheep clustered on the sides of the mountains and the rush of over-full waterfalls, my mind returned over and over to the hurt bound to my brain. I'll never be able to work while I'm in this state. I thought. I must get rid of the anguish.

'We'll stop for lunch, eh? Then I've got a surprise for you. Something you've always wanted to do,' he said.

'What's that?'

As he turned the corner I guessed as a signpost indicated the way to the Red Kite feeding station, at Gigrin Farm on the outskirts of Rhayader. After a rushed lunch we hurried to the farm, parked the car and onto the hide. At last I was going to realise a life's dream. I had always wanted to see the red kites and now it would happen.

A large group of us sat close together in the damp of the hide, ignoring our aching backs; strangers brought together by a shared purpose perching on the rough of wooded boards, staring through the gap of greenish-grey planks and out to a curved field that swept upward from our vision.

The ranger told us feeding time would be two o'clock today – 'Three o'clock in the summer as the birds don't have watches,' he said. We all laughed but I was focussed on my gaze. How would I recognise a red kite when I saw one? What made the red kite so different? Would we see anything at all as we were the only ones in the hide without binoculars? At precisely two o'clock a large tractor drew up a few yards away from the hide and a man alighted from the driver's seat and began to shovel vast amounts of pink meat chopped into small pieces out of the back of a pick-up onto the ground.

Again the ranger's voice intoned with red kite patter, that this has to be perfect beef – fit for human consumption, without any additives or hormones so that the birds remain as healthy as possible.

'They are hovering above us now,' he said.

I rubbed my eyes. Were those black specks what we were looking for?

'Not only will you see the red kites but also the buzzards trying to steal the food away from the kites and of course, there are the crows.'

I longed to look out from a pair of binoculars but the people who held them kept them clamped on their faces with no offer to borrow.

And then it began to happen.

'There's one,' someone shouted. I watched as a magnificent bird circled beyond our hide checking his safety and the temptation below. The crows like old men in black jackets landed and bounced on the ground, then assembled on the posts surrounding the field ready to steal and plunder; next to them an occasional buzzard with the same idea. More birds appeared in the sky. Still I was unable to tell and then one of the twitchers strung with cameras and two sets of binoculars sat forward, his large body straining for a better view. 'Look at the sky. It's full of them – there must be forty at least! Wonderful when you see that shaped tail – almost as if someone's cut a curve in it, isn't it?'

The dark dots barely visible transformed themselves into birds. Within the brightness of a grey-blue winter sky with a tired winter moon waiting to take over its duty, birds began to hover. There was no mistake now. Swirling above us, were vast creatures easing through invisible currents. They circled, first checking the terrain; scything through unseen wind-streams, curving a seamless course, wings extended touching heaven, almost motionless, held by magic – some miraculous artifice that was able to suspend these large birds, five to six foot across – with the mere flap of a wing. Then out of the sky, a hundred yards in front of us, they began to drop. Only for seconds, picking up the meat with an extended claw and rising with a few majestic movements of vast outstretched wings. As they rose back into the sky they transferred the spoil from claw to beak in a single motion – a piece of illusion – the perfect magic trick. And yes, red, looking like chestnut red stains on brown feathers. As they dived and swirled, the buzzards tried to steal the food from their claws and beaks. Airborne fights ensued. The daily Battle of Britain began; the kites the powerful victors. While the battles raged above, the crows took their chance stealing the last scraps below.

The ranger's voice intoned in another space, 'Of course they were almost wiped out. They used to exist in this part of the country centuries ago but were hunted almost to extinction by farmers and poachers and those who liked to see them dead and stuffed behind glass cages.'

And I continued to watch as the fights ensued and the birds made wider circles with their spoil, the battle over for another day. They circled for a few more times – the sky theirs – no boundaries to their horizons. And I thought of the majesty of the vision I had witnessed. I was privileged to see such perfection and felt humbled at the sight. But my emotions went beyond that simple gratitude, whispering a prayer of thanks that I was able to witness such splendour. Through those birds I realised that it is possible to restore the impossible; and even when a bird is declared extinct, it can return and live and exist where once it had vanished.

At that point I knew I had experienced an epiphany – a flash of overwhelming divine revelation that I must seek out and search for the positives. Like those birds when the odds seem impossible I too can allow my spirit to rise, achieve and pass painful boundaries. The birds were a metaphor for my life at that moment. I had to seek out the positives.

I hugged my husband.

'That was good wasn't it?' he said.

I stared at him with tears in my eyes, 'Perfect,' I said.

And on the return journey the radio played extracts from La Bohéme by Puccini and Zadoc the Priest and the Intermezzo from Cavaleria Rusticana and I sang each note, relishing the thought that there would be emails to answer and fresh work to tackle and a new and fascinating life would wait for me. That night I slept comfortably in my bed and woke without the unremitting sticky-winged terror of a nightmare. And the next morning my little grandchildren visited – eyes like scraps of a summer's sky and blond curls like Goldilocks. They sipped my soup. We played Snakes and Ladders, I gave them some new games I'd bought on the trip and told them the story of the huge birds I'd seen that held the sky between the breadth of their red-stained wings.

Lured by Boundaries

❧

Emily Hinshelwood

So, I forgot my waterproofs! I have 180 miles ahead of
me and the clouds are full udders. Black. But I've got my
red wellies and I'm going to start this journey even if it
means getting soaked to my knickers. Oh, the journey?
The Pembrokeshire Coastal Path. From which I'm going
to pluck poetry from the landscape. Who do I think I am,
Wordsworth or something? Although, I suppose he'd do
the whole lot in one go. Me, I'm going to take just as long
as it takes.

Okay, I'll come clean. As a child, walking for the sake
of walking never interested me. Nature happened far too
slowly; and what was so great about buds opening anyway?
Yes, I loved the urgency of ants yanking their eggs into
darkness when I lifted a stone or ducks bickering over
my stale bread, but being dragged out on a Sunday walk
seemed nothing short of sadistic. Besides, I had things to

do, I had to construct mazes for my hamster, and when was I going to write my 'books' if I was always having to 'get some fresh air'? But you know how it is – you have kids of your own, and suddenly it seems vital to inflict on them all the things you hated as a child. Like fresh air. And so the cycle continues, and I have developed a taste for walking.

15th April 2005: Amroth to Wiseman's Bridge

I've got my nose up against an Amroth groyne; sure there's a poem lurking in those salty cracks, those teeny tufts of algic hair, those wooden arms linked shoulder to shoulder. It's like chick culture, awash in a tide of cut-priced vodka. A cackle of cockettes studded with shells.

I must have walked about 50 metres, and I'm already unwrapping sandwiches – hissing open the flask, reassuring myself that I just need sustenance before cracking on. But everything wants to be noted. Half a Welsh flag clutters against a pole, a sunken forest groans beneath my boots. It all gets penned. For this is the start of the journey, and at the moment I have no idea what I will find.

People ask me if it is a pilgrimage of some sort? Is it an emotional discovery? Is it an awakening? I don't know. Does it need to be? I ask my subconscious difficult questions. But consciously I know it is nothing deeper than the wish to get away from the computer. And I've just read and been delighted with PennyAnne Windsor's collection of poetry based on the Parrett Trail and I want to do something similar. But, can I pretend? Can I make up an emotional discovery in order to hang my poems somewhere?

I go hopping across slabs of a timeline stretched out at Wiseman's Bridge – each jump a million years. The sea retires leaving an orange plastic glove, all order disrupted, and shells crawl along the beach in the wrong direction. There are little sand monsters with tails up like flags, a marker, a wind vein. Jeez, I don't have the vocabulary for this! Epiphany or no epiphany, I must buy myself a seashore book.

26th April 2005: Wiseman's Bridge to Tenby

I've been contemplating the concept of an awakening experience. Delving a little too far into the crevices in my head. I've discovered an amphitheatre of rock – all ready for performance. I've got this idea that – like Wordsworth – I could read the landscape as a reflection of my emotions. The sea chopsing and forever changing; thrusting flotsam at my feet; an arched bridge flooded, an orange buoy bobbing. Nothing static. Life disrupted and reassembled.

I'm eavesdropping – in the pub of course, jugs growing from the ceiling and lunchtime drinkers tapping at the bar to ABBA. Something strikes me about a snatched sentence, 'She sewed sequins on a dragonfly's wing' and I'm jotting conversations till I'm off again. A swathe of yellow sand walked with temporary artwork, the promenade lined with grey heads tilting at a helicopter. Even the gulls are curious. I'm on a bench in loving memory of Bill and Betty Hayter of Bridgend 'forever and always with us'. I wonder if they are here now – to help. It seems that there are words, flitting ideas dancing like fledgling birds, but what happens next? They don't open their wings and fly – they seem to plop on the page waiting for something, somewhere, to give them meaning.

13th May 2005: Tenby

Why did I start this? There's been no awakening to speak of, apart from just the joy of being out in a beautiful part of the world; the feeling of being lucky when everyone else is working. And tagged to that, the element of guilt at being so lucky which I try to suppress as much as I can. But the need for a defined journey is starting to weigh me down. It's pulling me away from the coastal path and into Tenby Museum.

If I thought it was hard before, now it is ten times harder. I am agog. I meet Jemima Fawr armed with a pitchfork fending off Napoleon's men, the teeth of cave lions, the likes of pirate Leekie Porridge. And I am awed by the raw notes of a student art exhibition. At sundown they have to throw me out. Now, my thoughts are ricocheting at tangents: art, history, geology. I sit looking out at Caldey Island, and breathe.

20th May 2005: Tenby to Manorbier

Just because…just because it's beautiful, the tall man bizarrely, top heavily stoops to pick a yellow cone shell from the sand. He sniffs it. The sea is so calm, there are no ruckles or wrinkles. Just oxeye daisies and the grassy tumble of bunnies. Rocks have crashed but that's in the past; they now stack like cards, and exude heat. Everything is in slow motion, except the snake which doesn't move at all; just lounges on the track, basking diamonds in the sun. My first snake – the deepest cut; I rescue it from the path. Don't realise it's an adder (till I get home).

I am still struggling with the first poem, starting to get demoralised about the whole project. A few days back, I was wondering how I could write a whole collection of poems about this edge; this hem – this sea on rock. But now I want to put in too much: Wales created out of sediment. On the edge of Iapetus Ocean – marine basin and lime-rich muds. We drifted north on a crustal plate. Then there were brachiopods, solitary corals, and we collided again, uplifted, folded, faulted and splayed. Our vegetational litter pressed below millennia. Then tetrapods, tree ferns, winged insects. On it goes before mass extinction 248 million years ago.

27th May 2005: Manorbier to Bosherton

These castles are as commonplace as traffic lights. Wales has more per square inch than the rest of Europe. But this one's romantic. I enter expecting at the very least to find a Welsh princess decked in crimson damask and a neck of pearls sucked from a barrel of oysters; or whole hogs spitted, brains rolled in breadcrumbs and gallons of monks' blood. I'd like to see the *tylwyth teg* on the lawn. But I don't. That would have been a discovery. But I am getting too bogged down in history for that. Delighted at being in the birthplace of Cambrensis, and wishing I could go back in time... to a non-battle day.

8th July 2005: Stackpole to Freshwater West

Yesterday, they bombed the double deck of a London bus; today I'm skirting tanks, trekking past barracks. A nod from a uniform behind barbed wire and it feels like war is everywhere. Through the scrub to the cut cliff, it is heavy quiet. Peaceful, but for horseflies that lunch on me, launching into flesh with blooded probosces and me slapping them dead. One step closer to the edge and silence breaks: Stack Rock packed like protestors in a park; the raucous din of auks and guillemots squeezed shoulder to shoulder, honking, hawking that the world will end.

I'm seeing circles everywhere. Flowers, lichen, rusted iron, warning signs 'No Tank Transporters'. I take photos. Not sure why I have been drawn to circles when it is a thin line I am walking. A line at the cusp between sea and land. Perhaps it's the daily cycle of sea being dragged in and out. In Paxton's baths the water was flushed out with every tide, taking all pus and ulcerous sores down the ocean's plughole. There's something contained in a circle

– still looking for hanger; wanting to define this walk.

29th June 2005: Freshwater West to West Angle Bay

It's going faster now. I'm putting aside the urge to find a reason for this journey. If I don't write any poems it doesn't really matter, but bizarrely as I am easing up, poems are writing themselves. Poems that I'm happy with, rather than being forced into an odd shape. A little boy has cut his hand on barnacles. For comfort he's been bought an ice-cream. But the blood is pouring raspberry ripple down his arm, all over his shorts, while his mother mops at the floor with napkins; and an old man regales us with stories of how he broke his leg and tied it together with an old washed up piece of rope before walking home.

20th July 2005: Angle to Pembroke

Public transport is getting dodgier by the day. Today it takes me six hours to get to the start of the walk. By the time I stagger off the final bus, I feel like I have eaten Pembrokeshire. I'm faced with oil refineries which look as out of place as spaceships; jetties like matchsticks, beermats balanced into piers, like playing card houses I used to make. There are chimneys puffing in every way I look, pylons crackling, and one tiny wind turbine.

18th November 2005: Pembroke to Milford Haven

I am now in the Milford Haven waterway with super-tankers, forts and gunhuts. There is in the air, a scent of bullying, where once, like a punch to an unsuspecting face, this stretch crumpled into rocky bays. Cut lips oozing rivers, bruised and swollen, headland crusted, cracked and pummelled to a point: here a spirit's song faltered and floated unnoticed onto outgoing waves. I am approached by a young lad being followed and taunted; I walk him back to school, amidst threats from his tormentors. It feels as though the cycle continues.

2nd December 2005: Milford Haven to Sandy Haven

In the Museum at Milford Haven, I meet Ray who steers me through corridors thick with history. I am so engrossed I want to accelerate the process and tip the museum into my head: From whale oil to crude oil. He makes me tea and I sit in Martha's Vineyard reading Wing Commander Ken McCay. This is where Nelson came with Lady Hamilton (oh, and her husband), to plan the Naval dockyard. I like the name – Aberdaugleddau – and picture two rivers kissing.

Now, a beast wades into the dock, with holds of black so heavy it could sink the world. It tips frail vessels, forces tide upstream, pushes salt into every crack, muffling, suffocating, tearing at banks; spills its load into vats and groans in buoyant release. The line between sea and sky is blurred. I shelter under the construction at South Hook jetty. More energy sloshing in. The clash of man and nature.

13th January 2006: Sandy Haven to The Gann

It's all stepping stones at low tide. Spent ages consulting the internet for tidal heights so that I can be here in perfect time. It meant quite a bit of running; writing notes on the go – I've never been good at spatial awareness, even with my trusty Brian John Trail Guide I'm teased by all these bays going in and out and up and down. It doesn't help that it's raining. Slapping me in sheets. The wind is so fierce it rattles inside my ears, flicks hair and whips gorse into my face. My cap is bolted so tightly to my head I can feel ridges develop across my forehead. My mac is flapping. I am rocked precariously across the path, mindful of the beware cliffs sign: man falling headfirst. Leafless trees lean away from the wind. My notebook is soaking. Friends ask why I'm still walking. I want to see the path in all seasons.

31st March 2006: Dale Peninsula

The poems are coming on. They seem to slide out of snippets of conversations or a delicate phrase from a book, or… well usually something quite separate from the coastal path itself. For example, today I've tugged Dorian Gray from the peacocks of Mayfair to the gale-force, fog-warned head at St. Anns. He in heavy furs, me in a mac from Millets. I showed him where the Sea Empress went down, though he couldn't see why I would mention the destruction of a beautiful coastline; or tell him how the first wave of cormorants slapped ashore. 'It was here she cracked', my mac flapping crow wings. The Empress tossed, supersized queen, all layers oozing, tugging at the harness in a delirium spurting unrefined slick, black blood pumping. Ten years ago, almost to the day.

14th April 2006: Dale to St. Martin's Haven

I've been so long inward-looking that there's a feeling of release when I turn west: out-ocean-faced, slapped by the salted wind, grabbed, urged, current-kicked. And today I'm walking through a conversation I wished I hadn't had. It's good to march on all syllables and let the ocean have it, though I miss half of what I'm seeing. I only read later about the Iron Age settlement.

28th April 2006: Marloes to Druidston

My favourite lecturer used to slide up the department in his Inuit socks; at parties wouldn't realise he was theorising with his wine glass on his head. It was he who taught me the exquisite lure of boundaries. The seam of sea on rock makes friction and fish dance in strobe light. Anything could happen. It is at the cusp that changes are made. You are defined by who you are not. Frances Bevans, in 1837 you were buried in St. Bride's Haven – on the cusp of adulthood. Now the tide uplifts your grave. Coastal erosion or the chance to re-dance the bay, and happen on strangers? Unscripted – it always is. Perhaps this is where I gain confidence in my project. It is starting to feel more fluid; easing up and I am enjoying the process of uncovering poetry.

9th June 2006: Druidston to Solva

The year is racing. Seasons unfolding at an alarming rate. I feel like I have missed spring. And now, the breeze deceives for when it stops I am clamped between hot sun and scalding sand – feet drag blended with landscape. A couple lie side by side like two half-baked tomatoes in a pan – drizzled with oil, turning now and then as though rocked and flipped by a master chef. My friend – a poet, a gentleman, a white-haired socialist – will die this weekend unexpectedly, and leave a hole. Around the corner, a wall of flowers is nodding, but I scratch through brambles, clamber chunky boulders and cut straight to turquoise. There are ferns uncurling. On emerging, I am caught by columns of flat stones balanced – piled single file like tributes. Without knowing why, I place a white, elegant rock on the top.

Sometimes reality is reflected in the landscape. And perhaps on a subconscious level we are in touch with different realities. There is no reason to search for explanations though it has a resonance deep inside when unexpected things happen. But I'm not the kind of person who looks for signs; I'd just like to note the quiver.

30th June 2006: Solva to St. Non's Bay

There are times when it is impossible to separate landscape from emotions. Sometimes the rocks sulk, and the islands lick their sandy wounds distant and aloof. Or sea's foam is dancing like fairies high in festival mood. I managed to walk passed The Vomit without reflecting on some new superpower trade laws that make me puke. But I struggled to get through The Pits simply because of the bad morning I had had. Today it is the adjournment of a public inquiry about a community wind farm I am involved in. And I can't shake my irritation. I've been stuck in the chamber too long with dead breath doing the rounds between 'yes wind farm', 'no wind farm and don't wreck a speck of my grass or the planet will shrink to pea-sized piss'. I've been stuck in the chamber too long with 'climate change poo poo', with 'nobody has a right to mess with my view', with 'what about the dead poet who loved this spot?' And I think, 'what about the living poet who loves windfarms?' They stand with their banners saying 'Save our Landscape'. But what about save our planet? New Orleans is the latest environmental disaster: Hurricane Katrina – 10,000 dead. Today I walk St Non's Bay – she who cured the eye yet now has the view of towers puking clouds up and outwards. The small community windfarm is refused planning. I throw a penny into Non's Well – after all she gave us David. Perhaps she'll sort out climate change as well.

30th October 2006: St. Non's Bay to Whitesands Bay

Looking at the map I'm expecting The Great Bitch to be a poem. It feels gutsy, gritty, some giant siren of an island just off Ramsey. In fact, I'm so caught up in thinking of Great Bitch that I'm only just noticing the beach at Porthlysgi strewn with what looks like gouged innards and shrivelled testicles. But when I round the bend and face Ramsey Sound, I am shocked to see I was wrong about the bitches. They're small, dare I say, innocent? Something unjust seems to have occurred, and I feel as though I've bought into the name calling. He lurched stern first, cracked his hull against her girth, tossed at the tide wits wild and undone till he washed up at the pub downed a round of jibe-talking jeering 'Where's your balls boy?' and he called her Great Bitch.

31st October 2006: Whitesands Bay to Llanrhian

I'm teetering on tilted rocks determined to reach the Head of this cracked and weathered landscape – Ice Age – in the tail end of a hurricane. Scrabbling, nearly crawling – half-human. I move like crushed ice and look out. There, a cormorant gashed and dashed up dead. Something about St David's Head scratches the surface off, so I'm left raw, with grazed elbows, spit flicked from my mouth, blinded by tears whipped into my eyes and deafened. There is never silence. W.G. Hoskins opens his book on *The Making of the English Landscape* by saying that poets make the best topographers. I have slid across these rocks, practically licked the contours, tripped over erratic boulders. Yes, W.G., I believe you're right.

1st November 2006: Caerhafod to Pwll Deri

I am no longer counting days nor do I have deadlines. I have developed an intimacy with the coastal path. I like to fantasize it belongs to me. I have circles coming out of my ears now; who knows what I will do with them. The end product is no longer important. It is the process that matters to me now. Engaging with landscape through words. Living.

2nd November 2006: Pwll Deri to Fishguard

I have finally popped the question after twelve years and me and my partner got married. For our honeymoon we could have brushed up elegant, nested in the Palm Court at the Ritz and pecked at petite pastries: all polish and highfaluting chatter. But we pegged our tent to the edge at Pwll Deri, like a mussel on a rock; watched the November sun plop into black and the start of the star-show free spectacular arch over us. We wedged the stove out of the wind, broke veg, threw lentils in, knocked back red wine from tin mugs and feasted clad in bobble hats, breathing out fog: elegant or what? It's got to the point now where all holidays and special events take place on the coastal path.

4th January 2007: Fishguard to Newport

I turn forty. Pass wintering trees: I like the idea of being half-way in life. I think I am slipping across the line from solid rock to fluid sea. It makes me smile. While the leggy ash races up smooth and tall; all-desperate for its buds to burst, the hawthorn – fuzzed with green-grey beard – plays with the wind – plucking, plinking thorns as master harpsichord. I had to nip into the Red Cross shop for gloves, and ended up lugging a full set of wooden handled cutlery. I try to take a short cut and end up catching the holy sister pegging out the convent smalls into a stiff breeze. A stone-white virgin Mary – chilled, mute and perfect – smugly gazes as I clunk against an icy padlock. If we were all made of stone we could sit solid on our haunches… promising.

I've mistimed this walk… again. And the sun has set. At first the intimacy is seductive, all senses alert. I feel my way; tactile and slow. Each squelch is that little bit more insecure. Could end up off the cliff like man falling headfirst. But night walking is quieter for some reason. The sea's peaks have a fluorescence that whisper, and water is pulled from side to side like lovers pulling covers. I am shifting my feet so slowly I think I have become part of the landscape. It is only when I see the lights of Newport that I see headlines in my mind's eye. Realise my vulnerability, not from nature. Sole walker at night. And it sits heavily.

1ˢᵗ February 2007: Newport to Moylegrove

I seem to have slipped through a crack somewhere. A frayed seam, slight rift, minor fault – nothing grand, but somewhere the line-ups don't match. Could have something to do with the concussion (large metal object fell on my head from a height), or the now-forty year old brain, or perhaps it is just that scratching between sea and rock that has led to cracks. At the brow of the hill, for a split second, I'm witness to post-battle clear-up: silhouettes in shock drag friends from ditches, bent to task, shoulders hunched push pull the steady cogs of war. Flooded with silence. I have gone back to a battle day – First World War?

I've not discovered time travel. It's a golf course. I realise that what I saw was complete fantasy; but however hard I try to shake that image it still stands in relief. Such a stark sight, it feels as though it has erupted from the core, crammed the cracks and cooled; it blots out the pretty coves and bubbling springs, and leaves a feeling of lost friends. But I suppose everything I have seen on this walk is fantasy. It is my interpretation of the landscape. And it is a pleasure to acknowledge this.

1ˢᵗ March 2007: Moylegrove to St Dogmael's

On the final walk I do the stile countdown – ten, nine, eight etc. to the last stile in St Dogmael's. I must have beaten the record for the slowest walker. It took two years. And I don't want to stop. The poetry collection is nearly finished, with no hanger to speak of except for being inspired by the coastal path. The circles have started to take over and are pushing their way into the collection itself. And if you can call it an epiphany I have realised that it is the walking that is the poetry. All I've been doing is picking moments of it, like plucking berries and preserving them on paper.

A Crow's Playground on Mynydd Hiraethog

Elaine Walker

Sitting in the round garden, I'm startled by a harsh bird cry close by and wonder if it's a goose, angling in low to descend on the lake in the valley. But I glance round to see a large crow, flapping its way heavily onto a fence post. It pauses a moment, to show its noble profile against the grey sky, before letting the wind lift it again to swoop over my head and down, following the curve of the hillside back into the trees.

It's a still day for this moorland where my home keeps a tenacious foothold in the face of regular high winds. But we've had heavy rain and gales for nearly a week and today they've stopped. Everything, everyone, breathes a long sigh, glad of the chance to stand upright for a little while and so I come outside, placing a blanket on a damp garden bench, with hat, coat and gloves against the cold, to sit and feel the air. The wind is slight but sharp against the back of my neck, bringing the familiar peaty scent of the moors and the green mould smell of wood and stone that need the warmth of some spring sunshine.

My two tiny call ducks are chirruping and chatting in the main garden, their sociable nature intrigued by my presence and irritated because they can't get out. I keep them penned in the main garden, where they have a pond and plenty to keep them busy, because if they inch a beak outside, foxes head here in droves. The ducks spend most of their time plotting an escape or trying to get in the house, where they spent one autumn morning sitting by the fire with Annie, the house-cat. In the summer, when the days are longer and foxes not so hungry, they can come in the round garden again, and I'll sort the fence out to stop them straying too far. They waddle off, bored with me now, to burrow eye-deep in a mole hill then raise beaks full of worms with their white faces dirty as though they've been eating chocolate.

Looking beyond the garden to the farmland and the moors, all the colours are muted. Even the sky is a cyclorama of murky grey billows stacked in layers, with just a surprising glimpse of blue over my left shoulder. The moors are that late winter brown-and-straw of old heather and matted grass tufts. The green patches here and there, attractive in their refreshing brightness, are bogs lurking to slurp up the unwary foot and fill its owner's boot with mud. Slowly over the coming months, the colours will change, turning to soft greens and tans dotted with the white tufts of bog cotton, but the moor always remains understated, keeping its secrets well hidden until they burst out in a late summer blaze of purple heather, visible for miles.

The round garden is slowly waking up – a few miniature daffodils have emerged, a little hesitant after some late snow, while the rowan and ash trees have hints of buds at their tips. Spring comes very cautiously here because winter can put in a last minute appearance right into early May. The stone wall I started last year reminds me I have work to do and that the round garden is far from finished. Well, there's not much point having a project if it's done in five minutes. I'd like to put in a wildlife pond and occasionally entertain ambitious plans about a stream. The raised beds I built last summer and protected with old window frames through the winter have survived well and already broad beans and cabbages are pushing at the glass. Each year I learn something new about gardening up here. I haven't yet decided how to tackle the collapsing bank or provide shelter from the gales that tear down the valley without losing the view of the moors. But today is still, so I don't have to worry about it and I can't do much in the garden until the ground dries out a little, so I'll just sit for a while.

A pheasant gargles in the dark green shelter belt of pines that stand out clearly against the soft moorland colours. It's an unusual bird for up here. For the first time in twenty-five years, there are at least three pheasants in the lane. I'm not sure what that says about the weather or the habitat or the pheasant population, except that during those years, a lot has changed. We used to have the first snow before Christmas – a sharp burst that was quickly gone, while the loft-filling, car-burying blizzards focussed on the time around my birthday in February. I saw that as a gift – I've always loved being snowed in. But the pattern has changed and now any snow at all before December is so rare that last year we went to Quebec in search of a white Christmas. Of course, while we were away it snowed here on Christmas Day, but this year it was mid-March before a flake appeared. Then it fell heavily for three weekends on the run, making up for lost time. Now this rain has washed away the last traces and left the landscape exhausted and sodden.

My horses are bored with eating hay in the shelters. I can see Darius and Topaz, their winter rugs caked in mud, as they take advantage of the break in the rain to get down to some serious grazing. Topaz has ripped the flap which covers his spotted Appaloosa rump and strands of his tail stick out through the tear, like a bad hairstyle. Darius has mud on his head. He always has mud on his head. In a clean summer field, I can find him lying flat out with his head pillowed on the only mole hill in sight. Little Jimmy, too furry to need a rug, is only tall enough for the black line of his back to show above the bank that encircles the round garden. J.B., herd leader and Jimmy's hero, ambles up to gaze at me over the fence, hoping I might have a carrot somewhere about my person.

On the yard, blue-eyed Mollie barks, disturbed by the distant sound of a car, while Steve peers at me under the gate, wondering how I can write without the help of a fine Labrador and why there have to be dog-free zones anyway. Once the echoes of Mollie's hysterical alarm call die away, I become aware of the birds. This is wild country and the small garden birds of the town are not that common. Instead we have skylarks and pied wagtails, siskins and curlews. Last year one of the outside cats caught a water rail, a bird I'd never even heard of before I found its sad little corpse in the shed with the donkeys looking at it. They'd never seen one before either, apparently. But we do have a single resident blackbird and a perky robin that dips into the shelters to help itself to bits of spilled horse and chicken feed. And mistle thrushes – for the first time last year, I saw a mistle thrush in the main garden, but the chaffinches that thronged there twenty years ago are strangers now.

There are plenty of crows, of course, noisy, opinionated and intelligent enough to look for help when times get hard. First there was Aoife, who I found badly injured and shouting for help, while I was riding. She spent three years living in the garden, demanding food and jumping on my shoulder to tidy my hair while I walked around the fields checking the horses. She was remarkably untroubled by horse noses snuffling at her feathers but she was a very self-possessed bird.

Then came Horatio, who turned up weak and exhausted by bird mites and just stayed on. He was never as bold as Aoife, but he would come to call, though I had to go inside before he would land for his food. He liked to hang out in the field with the horses, talking to them with such earnest enthusiasm that I was sure he had something important to tell them. I hope they paid attention. Occasionally, he went slug-hunting with the ducks and, if I sat very still in the garden, he would land in front of me and start preaching his message directly to me, his dark eyes fierce with intent. Then he'd return to his other mission, which was unfastening the copper wind-dancer that hung below one of his bird houses. He had three, because when he arrived he was very poorly and our garden is short of shelter so my husband made him three choices of sleeping accommodation, all of which he used depending upon the prevailing weather conditions. I like to think that he was the first crow in history to have a personal property portfolio.

My son came outside once, while I was putting out water and perches for Aoife to play on,

'Mum,' he said, 'This is a garden, not a crow's playground.'

Well, it started as a garden but when a crow moves in, things tend to change. We had to put a bolt on the yard gate to stop Aoife letting the dogs out and politely pretend we didn't mind Horatio's unpleasant caches of food tucked among the flower beds and in cracks on the concrete of the yard. Aoife's impression of a dog barking was good enough to send my son out looking for a stray and Horatio's preference for an early night meant closing the curtains in the living room at tea-time so the light didn't disturb him. Stored away in the gallery of my favourite memories is the day I took the dogs out on the moor with Aoife flying just above my head, barking all the way.

Both Aoife and Horatio outgrew their need of help and food over time and eventually flew off, strong and healthy, without a backward glance or a croak goodbye. But I'm pretty sure it's just a matter of time before someone new in a ragged coat of black feathers, injured or ill, comes limping in, demanding food, treatment and high-class accommodation.

This morning, there's a lot of birdsong in the shelter belts. After the rain, the birds are jubilant and a skylark suddenly wings overhead, swooping and plunging then heads high upwards, singing at the top of its small voice. The birds sound like a choral group with the stream which runs down the valley as their accompaniment. Unless you take the time to be still, or come out after dark, you hardly hear the stream at all, something I've never understood, because just now it sounds like some impressive waterfall.

The spiral movement of the wind-dancer, safe since Horatio left, catches my eye and the comical sight of two duck heads, bobbing up and down over the little wall beneath makes me smile. A noisy crow argument has started up in the pines and a wood pigeon coos in its midst, like someone trying to calm fractious children. Before long the cuckoo will arrive, we'll hear tawny owls at dusk, the merlin will reappear and maybe the hen harriers we spotted crossing our land just a few weeks ago will nest in the heather far out on the undisturbed moor. Then the weather will warm up and I'll sit at the top of the field in the long grass in the evenings with the horses mooching about, hoping to see a hare.

This is a strange place with its damp and fogs and severe winds. Winter lasts a long time, summer is short, spring and autumn just moments. It's not the best place to make a garden but whatever will grow here – flowers, horses, people – turns out strong and resilient. Since we've lived here, three sets of neighbours have left because they couldn't stand the wind. But I've grown to love it, and the moor's weather that settles like a cloak when it drops, so that the mist bring the hills near enough to touch and everything is hung with droplets of moisture.

Yet over the years, it has changed and maybe we won't stay forever either, though it's not the wind that might drive us away. The main road, an hour's walk away over the moors, seems closer than it once did. On a Sunday afternoon, the sound of motorbikes screaming at high speed along the straight line of tarmac that dissects the moorland is like a not-far-distant racetrack. And the ever growing wind farms get closer all the time. Even green energy has its price and, for anyone who lives out here because it is silent and remote, their relentless march in this direction can only be unnerving.

Maybe we will move somewhere lower down, more sheltered, where growing a garden doesn't mean checking every morning to see what has survived the overnight gales. We could trade the waning isolation for an easier life. But I'd miss being able to walk my dogs all day without seeing another person. I'd miss sitting among the heather on a hot summer afternoon watching the 'V' shaped wings of the hen harrier on the skyline. I'd even miss the wind and the lash of the rain on the windows when everything is safely battened down for the night and it's warm by the fire.

I gather up my coffee cup and blanket to head inside, but turn at the door as the birds fall into a breath-holding sort of silence. I recognise the nature of this stillness and look along the treeline until I spot a pair of buzzards heading down the valley, riding the soft breeze on outstretched wings. In a moment, a posse of crows will set out from the trees to see them off so the birdsong can start up again until dusk, when the rapid magpie alarm, 'Fox! Fox!' heralds the start of the night shift for owls and hedgehogs, while a slinky russet shape slips through the shadows.

The Welsh name for this moorland is 'hiraethog', and the root, 'hiraeth', means something like 'yearning' or 'heartsick for home'. It doesn't translate exactly, but I know what it means.

Trapped in Llethryd Swallet

❧

Maggie Cainen

My lamp beam fell on the black rocks – nothing to show our exit from the cave. My arrows, carefully scratched on the way in, had suddenly stopped. We were trapped deep underground in Llethryd Swallet with only an hour left on our caving lights.

Ignoring my shaking knees and thundering heart I struggled to stay calm. How would we find our way out now with no markings to guide us? I stared at Trevor in silence, furiously thinking, I'm sure I marked every step of the way in, so what on earth's happened? Did I accidentally erase the arrows squeezing past, or worse still actually forget to scratch one? We shone our lights in every direction where myriad dark patches looked like passages, but when we tried following them they stopped after a couple of feet or the roof dropped too low for us to penetrate. Time was running out on our batteries and the thought of being lost in the dark was terrifying me. Suddenly I was aware of how low the roof was, how far we were from the exit, petrified that tons of rock would smash down grinding us into the ground.

One of South Wales' last working miners, Trevor had been my caving buddy for many years, before he was transferred from Swansea to York's super pit. We've had some harrowing experiences together underground: abseiling, scrambling up and down waterfalls, forcing our bodies through tight squeezes and balancing along iffy traverses over vertiginous drops. Trevor's far braver than me on high ground but I'm more at home in water - we make a good team. Caving lost much of its magic for me after he left.

Llethryd Swallet, where I'd been marking the arrows, is a deep cave under North Gower, famous in caving history for rescues carried out with diving gear to evacuate trapped victims; its unpredictability adds to the danger because you need a long spell of dry weather to render the stream-bed approach safe. Once it floods, the whole lower passage to the inner chambers becomes impassable, and people have been holed up inside for days without light or food. The entrance lies through farmland, past a locked metal doorway above the stream, and then you have to wriggle head first down a steep boulder choke which can change on every visit.

We had started early one morning in late summer. First we had collected the cave key and written down our provisional itinerary and return time. We had parked in the field, donned wetsuits and heavy boots, attached our caving lamps and batteries, and stuffed a Mars bar under our helmets ready to explore Llethryd Swallet. That was my first and only visit to the cave so, as always, champion route-finder Trevor led the way, and I followed scratching arrows on the rocks pointing back towards the exit which I planned to erase on our return trip. At the bottom of the boulder choke we sat down and switched off our lights for a few minutes to help our eyes adjust to the dark. Excitement swept through me. I was anxious to get moving quickly to explore the fabulous cave. Its inaccessibility made it even more tempting. Despite the warm sunshine outside we shivered, with stream water dripping constantly onto us as we crawled down through the rocks. The natural light gradually disappeared the lower we went. The cone-shaped headlamp beam alters the shape of caves making every shadow look like a passageway. Spin 180 degrees and it all changes, impossible to recognise for the return journey.

We raced along the tight passage towards the main cavern, our headlamps highlighting the jagged black rocks which cut into my bare hands and poked through the holes in my wetsuit, leaving bruises in their wake. At times we were forced to our knees or even our bellies, our helmets knocking against the low roof, our noses full of the damp cave smell as we wriggled over obstacles. All real caves have a distinctive smell; it comes from the lack of natural light underground mixing with mud and stagnant water which combine in an unmistakable pungent aroma. You won't find it in floodlit show caves, it's been sanitised away. There were no 'pretties' to see en route that day, such as cave flowers, stalactites or rare, sideways-twisting heligtites, just mud, stones and wet rock and all the time the noise of the distant underground river rumbling in our ears. I was just thinking the first part would never end when abruptly we reached a steep mud bank from which dangled a few feet of frayed rope. We couldn't rely on it holding as we slipped and slithered endlessly back down the slope trying over and over again to get a purchase on the viscous mud which stuck to our boots weighing them down. After half a dozen tries Trevor finally made it on top of the bank. Spread-eagled across it he leaned down and hauled me up to join him. We sat astride the mound catching our breath, utterly spent.

'It's even harder going underfoot inside,' warned Trevor. 'It's very boggy. Whatever you do don't fall down - we'd never get up again in all that mud.'

Despite the overpowering stench of cave mud that clogged our noses, our first sight of the huge grotto took our breath away. The roughly L-shaped cave stretched forever, soaring impossibly high. Our caving lamps were too feeble to penetrate to the far side and dwindled away to nothing. It felt strangely surreal, like discovering a new world. Curtains of fine mist hung in the damp air adding to our sense of disorientation. Delicate icicle stalactites clustered overhead, but poor visibility stopped us examining them properly. We caught tantalising glimpses of flowstone calcite formations, towering columns and tapering knotty stalactites and stalagmites, many streaked brown with mineral deposits, but most creamy white. Underfoot the slick sludge clung to our boots, making us sink to above our knees as we blundered our way across. It felt like quicksand sucking at our feet, dragging us down to the foul-smelling depths of the uneven ground. The only approach to the amazing sights was to claw our way over to an elevated ridge round the edge. Every step was exhausting, our boots made obscene sucking noises as we heaved them up from the clinging mud over and over again. We were shattered before we'd even entered the second cavern, but keen anticipation drew us on. Time was running out. We felt we were the first discoverers of the cave, as we made our way gingerly around the edge of the huge L-shape, the only sounds our panting breath and distant running water. Damp permeated the air, creeping under our wetsuits, which already dripped with sweat.

In the second cavern through the mist our lights revealed further elusive sights of stalactites and stalagmites and we gazed in silence at the wonders of nature creating such beautiful objects drip by drip over thousands of years. Most of the stalagmites were uneven, bulbous shapes like knobbly walking sticks or fat little gnomes but I remember too, some elegant fan-shaped stalactites and a huge brown column. The mist gave them a dreamlike quality. I longed to get closer to examine them one by one but I knew I mustn't touch, especially as we were mired with mud from our helmeted heads to our muck-clogged boots, and we shrank from accidentally damaging what had taken millennia to create. I knew of few cavers who had penetrated through to the second chamber and we had little time to explore properly as the trip had taken far longer than we'd planned. We stood awestruck at the second entrance afraid to venture into the bottomless mud covering the ground.

Soon we had to make our way back because we had only signed out for eight hours and our lamp batteries were near their limit. We had to return the key by seven thirty to signal our safe return. It was considered the ultimate disgrace for experienced cavers like us to have to call out the rescue squad if we forgot the time or got lost. Injury was another matter, but I'd still asked my husband to ring the caving club if we weren't home by eight.

Years later I can still feel that rough grit savaging my broken fingernails, as we followed the arrows wriggling our way towards the exit through the tight holes, sometimes on bruised knees which felt every pebble despite the wetsuit's thick neoprene, and sometimes flat on our bellies when the roof dipped too low. My shoulders cramped with contorting them through sharp squeezes.

So now here we were stymied: no scratched arrows to guide us, no cave survey to consult and both our time and light were running out. Always the leader, Trevor could see how frightened I was as the elation of seeing the huge stalactite cathedral seeped away.

'Don't worry, Maggie, we must have missed it because we were rushing. You have a rest whilst I go on and check for possible ways out, there might be more than one.' So, ignoring his own fatigue he went ahead searching countless false leads branching off the narrow passage to the left and right, but each one ended impassable with his helmet jammed against the roof. My turn next, slimmer than him I was able to push further along the gritty, airless spaces which pressed down on me but when I had to remove my caving helmet to penetrate deeper into the final, most promising one, I realised I was on the wrong track. It was a sobering moment. The full enormity of what was happening hit us both. We were lost and would probably have to stay there for hours and we'd be lucky if anyone found us before our lights gave out as no-one knew exactly where we were. Adrenaline surged though our bodies. Even Trevor's face paled under the mud with sweat pearling down his cheeks. He was the calmest person I knew, steadfast in all situations. A miner all his working life he'd survived being trapped for days in cave-ins in the coal mines. I was amazed that his hobby was caving as well as his livelihood. Now panic threatened us both. I was shocked that my normally unflappable buddy was feeling the pressure too. Having to return the key by seven thirty made the situation worse. We sat in the middle of the narrow passage utterly dejected after the huge high of our trip, aware that we'd less than an hour of full beam left on our caving lights, with no idea how to find the passageway which led to the unstable boulder choke back to the surface. Suppose it had been raining outside causing the stream to fill up and flood the passage? We'd have to take things slowly in the choke or risk breaking a limb if we penetrated at the wrong angle and sent the boulders tumbling. What if the rocks had shifted whilst we'd been exploring the caverns? We'd never find our way out safely and we'd be trapped down there in the dark until the cave rescue squad turned out mob-handed to search for us several hours later.

Eventually Trevor decided we should both backtrack towards the big cavern and start again; it was excruciating, our bruised knees protested, pain cramped our backs and tiredness threatened to overwhelm us as we crawled on all fours over the spiky stones. We were starving hungry, our fried breakfast a distant memory. We'd eaten our Mars bars hours earlier, and we'd even exhausted our emergency tube of glucose sweets. We worked our way backwards to the dangling rope end and started again, checking every arrow. At first it went well as we spotted each mark which luckily I'd omitted to erase, but suddenly they stopped.

We cast our eyes in every direction, sweat pouring from us, hearts racing. My whole body shook with exhaustion; hunger gnawed at my belly, despair was close. Tears were starting in my eyes when Trevor shouted 'Look Maggie,' pointing at the roof a metre above our heads. We could just make out a tiny arrow going straight up and the dark shadow of a hole. We'd made the elementary error of forgetting that caves go off in any direction not just to the sides but through the roof and floor as well. Now when we thought about it we realised that it'd been quite a drop to access the lower passage, but at least I'd remembered to scratch the arrows. Tiredness, hunger and panic forgotten we fairly flew along to the exit, locked the door, jumped into the car still in full muddy caving kit and signed the key back in with minutes to spare.

The Spirit of the Teifi

※

Sarah Boss

Where the estuary of the River Teifi starts to broaden out, before it flows into the sea beneath the cliffs at Mwnt, the town of Aberteifi, or Cardigan, stands on the north side of the water. Prominent on the bank at Cardigan is the church of St. Mary, and the legend connected with that church tells us of the holiness of the river that flows past it.

An old tradition recounts that a statue of the Virgin Mary was washed up on the shore, and in the Virgin's hand there was a lighted taper. Now this was a miraculous taper, which burnt continuously without ever being consumed. So the local people built a shrine for the statue, Our Lady of the Taper, at the place where it had been found. There the sacred flame continued to burn for nine years, until a man broke an oath which he had sworn upon it; and then the candle went out. But pilgrims continued to visit

Our Lady to seek favours, such as the healing of ailments, and the shrine became the great church which still stands on the Teifi bank. There was a similar tradition at Haverfordwest; and in the Oxfordshire town of Burford, it used to be said that the spirit of a seventeenth-century lady of the manor would ride down the river carrying a lamp. The river at Burford is the Windrush, whose name is from a Celtic root, *wenrisc*, meaning 'fair water', or 'sacred stream', and I wonder whether all these traditions date back to an ancient British belief that each river had a presiding goddess, or was itself a deity. Certainly, Our Lady of the Taper is the presiding spirit of the Teifi.

When I came to live on the banks of the Teifi, it was not at the river's mouth that I settled, but far upstream. As the year descended to its black-frosted depths, and the hibernating sun made room for the crystal clarity of a winter's moon and the spangle of the Milky Way, I came to make my home near the village of Cwmann. And the place I came to was enchanted. True enchantment is said to be close to holiness, and there was something heavenly about this place – something quite other. The natural world, through the seasons of the year, gives an inkling of eternity, and there are certain places where nature seems almost to make eternity present in this world of time and change. There are places in the Teifi valley where the silver birch, the brook and the swan all seem to be more than themselves, yet more truly themselves. These woody, watery, feathery inhabitants can become almost translucent, delineating an Otherworld, which shines through them like sunlight on stained glass. And the ancient way which leads along the Teifi from Cwmann to Tregaron is holy land of just this kind.

The farmhouse where I lived at that time, Felindre Isaf, is set on the ground which rises to the east of the river, above the road skirting the edge of the flood meadows. In summer, sheep and cattle graze in the fields; but when there is heavy rainfall in winter, the river's banks disappear under a lake-like expanse of water, which most people see from the causeway that leads onto Lampeter Bridge. From my bedroom window at Felindre, I would watch the river rising, and see the sunlight reflected on the floodwaters.

The source of the Teifi is not many miles from there, and all the river's tributaries rise in the hills close by, so whenever it rains hard, it is not long before the water level gets higher. A broad stream tumbles down the hillside past Felindre. It trips and bubbles its way under a stone bridge, and down through the pastures to the channel that will guide it to Cardigan, and out to the Irish Sea. The mill house from which Felindre takes its name still stands there, and it was from this broad, bubbling stream that the mill race was once diverted.

From the first time I came to Felindre – when I could scarcely believe that I might live in such a treasure of a place – I knew that the land carried some special blessing. It was a place of enlightenment and healing. When I had been living there for a short while, I started to reflect on how ancient the road must be that runs past it. There was no bridge where Lampeter Bridge now stands until Steffan, the Norman lord, built one. I suppose people would have forded the river in summer. But the river crossing that the Romans had built was upstream, at Llanfair Clydogau. To reach Llanfair on a journey westwards from the Cambrian mountains, one would have to take a northward detour along the road up the east side of the Teifi, past where Felindre now stands; and travelling eastwards, one would come south to Cwmann by the same route. The name 'Llanfair' means Marychurch, or St. Mary's, and I wonder whether this dedication is connected with the ancient bridge, since it was once common for bridges to have chapels on them, and most of these were sacred to the Virgin Mary.

This road along the eastern bank of the Teifi must have been walked by St. David himself – Dewi Sant – since another of the villages along its way is Llanddewi Brefi, where, according to tradition, the ground rose up under David as he preached, forming the hill on which the church now stands. David would have heard the mewing buzzards, as I did; he would have seen a rook trying to drive one off, and the bird of prey descending upon its tormentor. To David, these would have been symptoms of the world's fallen condition – of the fact that God had intended all creatures to live in harmony, but, when Adam and Eve ate the forbidden fruit in the Garden of Eden, all nature was cursed and went awry. Yet would he not also have been intensely alive to the blessings that still burst forth in each leaf and every breath of air? I remember walking up the road through Cellan, the hedgerows and trees giving forth densest greens, bejewelled with blues, whites and pinks, and I remember feeling a contentment that would have saved Adam and Eve from wanting anything more than their present joy in the Garden. One sunny evening at the end of May, I went dancing in Cellan with a group of friends; and as I gazed at the setting sun, and the glowing colours of hawthorn and oak, and the maple and horse chestnut in village gardens, the air was heavy with holiness.

The land there is always so alive. I had never seen so many swallows, or been as close to them, as I was in the first week of May at Felindre. Sometimes, I would open my curtains in the morning and see a great spotted woodpecker on the telegraph pole, or a red kite on the branch of a tree. At night, I would hear owls hoot and squeak, and other sounds from birds and animals that I didn't recognise. In the evening, rabbits would come out to dine in the field in front of the house, and would allow me – though nobody else – to get quite close to them before they scampered back to their burrows. Nearby, on an old bank beneath the garden of a modern bungalow, I found wild flowers which I had never seen before, and discovered that they were pale toadflax: delicate whitish cups of flowers, with mauve markings.

Very late in the spring came lambing, and the night air was filled with bleating; and in the daytime a lamb would occasionally escape from its field and cry in pitiful distress when it could not find its way back in again.

One Sunday morning, the shepherd came with his dog,

as usual, to move the flock from one field to another. This was a procedure in which the sheep frequently offered little co-operation – not, I think, because they were badly disposed towards man and dog, but rather, because they were uncertain as to where exactly they were meant to be going. On the morning in question, however, the flock as a whole were being successfully driven between some outbuildings, when one ewe held back and refused to follow. The dog, a lively border collie bitch, ran around the recalcitrant sheep, and suddenly the two animals were up on their hind legs, each with its forelegs against the other's shoulders, like two stags locking horns. The sheep was much larger than the dog, but the dog was more nimble. The dog drew back, and, with her nose, biffed the sheep in the shoulder. The ewe rolled over onto her side, as the bitch stood behind her and barked a command. The ewe then got up and followed the flock; but I was delighted to have seen such independence of spirit.

On another Sunday, however, when the shepherd brought winter feed to the flock and the sheep all gathered round to get stuck in to the new supplies, I noticed there was one who ran out of the field and did not re-join the rest until the shepherd and dog were departing. I wondered whether this was the same sheep who, on a previous occasion, had refused to do as she was bidden. If so, then she may have been motivated less by independence of spirit than by fear. Perhaps she sensed something of the fate that had befallen her lamb at the slaughterhouse a few miles away.

The hills of mid-Wales are over-grazed. The sheep demolish the heather and bilberry, leaving bracken to take over. New house building in the village of Cwmann is gradually crossing the fields in the direction of Felindre. Our absurdly high standard of living is destroying the land upon which it depends: we are not biting, but devouring, the hand that feeds us. Yet in West Wales, at least, it may still not be too late. To put it in language that St. David would understand: we have time to repent. Living at Felindre always filled me with hope.

A Chinese friend recently told me that, according to the principles of Feng Shui, the ideal location for a house is one which has mountains rising behind, and a river flowing in front. This describes precisely the setting of Felindre, and to me, it was ideal. After work in the evening, I would walk home across Lampeter Bridge in the light of the sun as it set across the broad green valley; or in winter, following the road towards Cellan, with the street lights disappearing behind me, I would feel the gentle shadows enfold me, in misty rain or beneath a starlit sky. I'd walk through the mud up the drive, and before going in through the front door, I'd turn round to marvel at the mountains and the river or the glittering heavens. In the morning I might find a badger's paw print in the ice. When I left Felindre to move into Lampeter, I thought my heart would break.

Yet I know that the spirit of the Teifi flows on, wherever I am. I know that spirit as Our Lady, and for all the time that I lived at Felindre, I was certain that she was also the spirit of the rock on which the house was built, and of the land surrounding it. People know this Spirit by different names, but all can honour her by showing reverence for the river and the soil, both in Wales and across the whole earth.

The Rock Pool

❦

Dee Rivaz

I was born in Cumberland, but by feeling I am from Wales, where we moved when I was eighteen months old, in 1954.

My mind runs over my earliest memories, feet unsteady along the path, following my sister through the woods of Wern y Wylan, down past dry stone walls to the shore. Our sandals flap over uneven, smooth-washed pebbles, metallic from the sun and passing feet. Curlews shrill over the windswept marshes.

In the meadow, through the gate, is a speck; in the distance something brown, spider-sized. My sister tugs me on, 'Come on, keep up!' My climb is hard and teetering, over the gate. What is that spider-sized speck? Is it a cow or a bull? I don't know; I don't care. I'm scared of the drop from the top of the gate. She takes us closer. Then a bit closer, just to find out. Just to know. Imagine the sound of soft thundering growing until a flicker of menace becomes the certain nightmare of pursuit. 'Run!'

My small, three year old cognitive intelligence has no reference for 'bull', for this hurtling nightmare that is to haunt me nightly for years, for this chip of landscape that detaches itself and attacks.

I remember my own pursuit of Olwyn, into the hills, braving the geese and gander to find him, following him to fetch in the sheep. 'You've missed one,' I insist, pointing to another speck in the distance, this time a sheep needing rescue: 'Da iawn, Bach!' I trot back with him to the farmhouse to get tinned peaches and evaporated milk for my reward. I want nothing more than to be lost with him in the hills, forever.

But we moved when I was four, to the other side of Anglesey, where the marshes gave way to cliffs and coves. Ravenspoint, Trearddur Bay, on Holy Island. Here my parents managed the extraordinary place that had evolved from private house, through post-war convalescent hospital, to hotel.

To begin with we lived in whichever rooms were not booked or bookable for a while: a strange, nomadic game. But my playground was acres of headland, cliffs and three beaches of utterly different secrets and treasures, all mine. My mind and body as one were occupied with gaining knowledge of those places. Recalling it now makes my palms itch and the soles of my feet tingle. My parents were preoccupied with the hotel, my sisters mostly away at school, the staff of the hotel were busy with the guests;

until I too went away to school, I was often alone.

Come spring, my feet needed training for the barefoot summer ahead: could I run across the gravel without crying? It was necessary to find some sort of superiority to the Cheshire nouveau riche, the Liverpool merchants and their gold shackled wives, and to the white socked sailing club crowd, whose commodore hats and deckshod arrogance made me feel invisible.

Come early summer I was aloof in my parallel universe where I was able to see, able to hear, able to touch and to taste what the tourist buffoons could only snap or dab at with their cameras and brushes.

They tramped down to settle into their paraphernalia of blankets, windbreaks and windcheaters, whilst I stalked, near enough naked, into the bone crushing chill of the Irish sea. I'd strike out in a wild dog-paddle for my own island, where the rocks received my toes like old friends, and I could run up to the soft scratching of thrift and lichen to stand akimbo and watch the poor fools, impostors, ants and dolls lined up in their uncomfortable groups, well above the tide line.

Yet I would long for their company, envying something – I was never quite sure what. I settled for despising their tenant status in my home, yet was resentfully grateful, like some poor relation, when I got asked along on an expedition or dashed a piece of fruit from a picnic here and there. I would envy Llewelyn too, the old man who rowed standing up, dogged and unhurried, crossing the bay to check his pots, ignoring all of us. I envied him because he didn't care.

But I could show the children where adders slept in sun drunken bliss. I could take them to a bath hidden in the cliffs where, legend had it, Sir Henry Grayson walked towel in hand, for his daily salt-bath therapy. I could show them where Jane, the ship's figurehead, reared bosomy and proud from her retirement in the rocks. I could take them for a ride on the sphinxes crouched in absurd white marbled splendour either side of the drive. I had treasures buried in the warren of a hidden garden, where you could bounce and roll on thick mattresses of thrift. I had a castle of my own, a small folly, with real turrets and a stinking room below, that might have been a dungeon. I could point out the dark and glowering house across the bay where they filmed Wuthering Heights. I could take my kitten for rides on the stone ravens by the gate. I could swim in an aged pool built into the foot of the cliffs whose slick, ceramic walls were cracked and fell away to fathoms of dark water and menacing, feathery shadows of weed.

My small body was innocent of so many lurking dangers below, above and all around, and yet I was intuitively, purposefully afraid most of the time: it kept me safe. My native wit was fashioned by the landscape.

I fished in rock pools for the soft, pulpy, goggle-eyed blennies and gobies. I harvested shrimp and winkles and boiled them in a billy can for frustrating, painstaking feasts. I knew how to pick off heads and shells, and fish out the tender spirals of flesh with a pin, and I could find cowries: tiny disembodied mouths, more precious than gold.

My parents moved from Wales in 1964, when I was eleven. For thirty odd years I found no match for the ragged Holy Island coastline, I felt nothing so warm as the Anglesey summers, nor little as wild as the island winds that set a froth as thick as snowfall on the lawn, and I saw few sights as breathtaking as Snowdonia across the straits from Beaumaris. And when I found my way back to that turning, up the side of Trearddur Bay to Ravenspoint, I had to stop while my childhood self raged out to beat me with the fury of desertion. And I could not say where I had been, for it seemed to me that I had been nowhere.

Although it is so easy for me to go there now, I seldom do. And when I do take the road up to where the hotel once stood, when I teeter across the pebbles to the sea, that lonely child regards me now as she would any summer visitor. She sniffs in contempt as she watches me recoil from the icy water, then turns and bounds back to her look-out post on the cliffs.

Diary of a Winter Afternoon

❦

Sue Anderson

3p.m. I set off with my son to climb the Buckholt. He is carrying a video camera. As an artist, he wants to record the sunset. I'm empty-handed: I want to record the experience. The Buckholt is a high point on the edge of Monmouth. It's not a mountain, not even a hill, just the end of a high, wooded ridge, but it has its own magic. 'Buckle for witches,' the old rhyme goes.

To the west are the shifting shapes of the Black Mountains, deep in the Welsh countryside. They weave and turn as we walk, now the Blorenge, now the Sugarloaf, now the Skirrid.

To the east is the Welsh border. We are so close to that zigzag line, that as we make our way through the woods to the top of the ridge, we will cross and re-cross it, slipping between countries. There's a feeling of being on the edge, in two places at once, in no place at all. We're poised at the turn of the year, in the misty no man's land between night and day, walking the path between past and future.

3. 15pm. We tramp up the rutted lane, between the bare trees and winter hedges, and as we go we talk about recording. Ben says that in the future, there will be a machine to capture not only sights and sounds, but smells and sensations. As he stops to make a digital memory of the winter sky, I'm trying to record the moment in my head, to store against the time when he will be miles away.

Long shot – deep to pale blue sky. Dark outline of mountains. Pale lemon sun.

Close up – a tall young man in an old jacket and thin jeans, pale with cold, mind fixed firmly on his task.

3.30 pm. He plays a bit of the film back. Shows me the things you only notice on tape – faint echoes of birdsong – a bit of bark on a tree. I notice his face and hands. He studies the light on the tree trunks – pink tinge, then gold. I see the road in the distance, measuring out the time we have.

3.40pm. A line of houses. Dogs bark through the hedge and he points the camera at them, at the trees, at the dying sun. I give him my gloves; his hands are freezing and I can use my pockets. Now the hedge is blocking the view. We have to get up on the ridge before the sun disappears. We start to walk faster. I go ahead as he stops again, caught by some detail. Now I am alone, on future walks, thinking back to this one.

3.45pm. We turn off into the woods. He points the camera.

Close-up – Snow in patches.

Close-up – Mud underfoot.

We climb the path up the ridge. The sun is sinking behind the trees. Now we are twisting, turning, out in a lost land with no grip on geography.

3.50pm. Just in time. There is a glow, spreading like molten metal over the mountains. For a few seconds, glory blazes, then the sun is gone. Just a memory, a yellow band on the horizon, and the pink tinge of sculpted clouds behind the mountains.

Now the urgency is over, he takes time to show me how to work the camera. I pan the horizon, dark red and heavy yellow burning through the viewfinder. It could be dawn, I think. Except that the moon is nudging my shoulder, bright silver behind the pines.

I turn the camera on my son. Each time he comes home, he's different, seems taller. Each time he has more and more memories I don't share. That's as it should be. I hand the camera back.

4.00pm. We slog on along the ridge, determined to reach the end, filming every step. Ruins of brambles, still bearing wizened fruit, take me back to summer. As we reach Buckholt Top a vista of sprinkled lights rises to meet us: the town, far below. I turn to Ben, moon on my right now, ghost of sun on my left, and watch him try to capture it all.

4.15pm. We set off back down to the road. It's darker now, but still with that peculiar dawn-lightness from moon and sun combined. The way seems longer; the path more slippery. Ben, still filming, takes a step off the path into the trees. And he's gone. That's what darkness can do. Two steps and you disappear. Maybe a witch has taken him. Then I hear his voice, whistling notes into the microphone, making sound effects. I peer into the shadows and see a darker smudge with the red spark of the recording light.

4.30pm. Barking dogs. Human voices. The main track again. Now the moon is spectacular, a blazing disc. But just as I think this, it switches off. A row of pines has cut in, bringing blackness. The path fades away beneath my feet. The whistles and calls are behind me now. Snatches of voice, edges of sound.

Through the trees, I catch the pale glow of light. The moon is there again, picking out laced branches across the deeper blue, with stars twinkling between. On and on. Are we getting anywhere? We could be lost, going in circles. Then I see moonlit fields in the distance. Ben behind me, still filming, seems in no hurry, untroubled by the darkness.

4. 45pm. The gate to the lane. We're out of the woods. The road is lit by pools of moonlight shining between trees, like street lamps. In one garden someone has covered the bushes with Christmas lights. Then, better than that, comes a tall tree whose branches are tipped with gold from the dying sun.

As we approach the main road into town, there is a sound behind us: a single, long howl. It's coming from the woods. Is it a fox? Maybe it's someone calling goodbye. My son puts his camera away and we talk again. He will be gone tomorrow and this walk will be a memory. I watch it through my mental viewfinder, hoping some of it might stay, as we pick our way through the potholes, back home.

All at Sea

❧

Jackie Williamson

'Can you take the tiller for a bit while I go and reef the main?' asked my husband, Mike, giving me no time to refuse. I obediently slid into the yacht's driving seat as he lurched along the coach-roof to start getting the sail down. Sharp needles of rain mixed with stinging salt spray, the wind howled with vindictive ferocity, Cevamp – our small wooden sailing yacht – was bucking like an unbroken bronco, and my co-ordination went completely haywire. I had never found it easy to steer into the wind. This time it was impossible.

'Can't do it, can't do it,' I moaned miserably to myself, my stomach churning in terror at the sight and sound of the big white sail flapping crazily in all directions as the violent tossing of the boat caught every gust. Each time the wind snatched at the canvas the heavy boom slammed over the cockpit and cannoned across to the other side, stopping with a juddering crash that yanked on the rigging and made the yacht shudder. The main-sheet snapped free of its retaining cleat on Cevamp's stern and whipped at my head and ears before snaking away over the back of the boat. As I tugged the heavy rope back in, Mike wrapped one arm around the cold aluminium of the mast and struggled with his spare hand to release the main-halyard so he could lower the sail. He is a strong man but I knew he wouldn't be able to hold on for long, before the wildly swinging boom sent him flying into the raging water. The noise was deafening. Wind and waves conspired to shut out all other sound and as Cevamp heeled further and further over, the top of the mast threatened to dip into the waves. I hung on tight to the tiller, hugging it close against my body in a desperate bid to straighten the boat. Frantic, I looked up at Mike and saw his lips moving as he tried to communicate something to me.

'Pardon?' I yelled, polite in spite of my fear. His lips moved again, but the wind tore his words away almost before they left his mouth.

'What?' I yelled back, pitting my full strength against the force of the tiller. By now Cevamp was heeling at an impossible angle and the sea was tumbling over the gunwales, swamping the cockpit and gushing through the companionway into the cabin. I was glad Mike had insisted on me putting on my safety gear but he'd removed his harness to go up to the mast and now he was struggling to keep his footing. The power of the waves against his legs and ankles threatened to sweep his feet from under him and he was having real trouble holding on. The boat was no more than a fragile matchbox, crashing up, down and sideways into the huge foaming breakers which were coming at us from all directions. By now I was really frightened. I desperately wanted to do the right thing. I was terrified Mike would be swept overboard, and I would be to blame. My knees were weak and shaking and my heart was pounding so hard that I could almost hear it over the noise of the storm. Using a peculiar logic, and as much muscle power as I could muster, I pulled the tiller harder and harder towards me, hoping this would pull the boat back up and onto an even keel again. I was so frightened I couldn't think straight and I failed to realise that my actions were having the opposite effect, tipping the boat even further over onto her side. I was overwhelmed with panic. By now, not only Mike's lips were moving, he was also gesturing frantically with his free arm, still hanging on grimly to the mast with the other. I was incapable of understanding, powerless to act and convinced I was about to consign him to a watery grave. My heart stopped pounding and sank altogether. I was pretty sure by now that I wasn't doing what I was supposed to be doing, but didn't know what else to do.

'I still can't hear you,' I wailed, holding ever more tightly onto the tiller and wondering how long it would be before the mast actually went under the water.

'Steer into the wind,' yelled Mike over the slamming of the sea and the slapping of the sails. No response.

'Steer into the wind,' he yelled again. Still no response

from me. I could only watch, frozen in fear, as the end of the boom dipped into the waves and Mike's booted feet began to slide from under him.

We'd known even as we sailed out of Pwllheli a few hours earlier that, despite the brightness of the day and the warm sunshine on our backs, bad weather was on its way. The first clue came from Holyhead coastguard station: north westerly gale force eight, imminent. The second came twenty minutes later on the Radio Four shipping forecast: winds north westerly six to gale force eight, showers.

As the late afternoon gave way to early evening we could see from the way the waves were building and the frequency of white caps on their crests that there was already a good force five powering us along. The wind was picking up too, so while I made doubly sure that everything was secure on deck and stowed away in the cabin, Mike furled in the genoa, put a couple of reefs in the mainsail and started the engine.

'What do you think?' he said. 'Shall we keep going round the headland for a bit longer to see whether we can get across Hell's Mouth to Aberdaron, or should we just cut our losses and go back to Abersoch?' He always asked me for my opinion, knowing full well that I invariably relied on him to make the decision.

We were en route for Anglesey where we planned to go harbour hopping, but we were already several days into our two week holiday. I really wanted to take the easy option and go back to Abersoch but I knew Mike wanted to press on and heard myself saying, 'We'll cross Hell's Mouth. Why go back when it seems reasonable enough to go on?'

An hour later we were approaching the western end of Hell's Mouth on the rugged coastline of the Llŷn peninsula. The waves were bigger than ever and the earlier sunshine had given way to a sullen orange glow that was partially obscured by silver-edged black clouds flying overhead.

Suddenly the squall hit us. Spray everywhere, howling wind, huge waves and stinging shafts of rain. Mike decided to get the mainsail down to relieve the stress on the yacht but as he handed the tiller over to me with a terse instruction to head into the wind, Cevamp heeled right over. I lost my nerve. I could see Mike was in danger of being tossed overboard and battled to hold the tiller. As he fought to keep his grasp of the wet mast I knew that unless I took control of myself our position was a grim one. Either I gave in to my panic and put both our lives at risk or I got a grip of myself, kept my head and did whatever it took to get this boat back on an even keel.

I still don't know how it happened but something, a primeval survival instinct perhaps or adrenalin-charged awareness, snapped me out of my frozen state. Mike's repeated instructions in the past had, it seemed, finally sunk in and I let go of the tiller. The effect was instantaneous. Cevamp straightened up sufficiently for Mike to be able to get the sail down while I nonchalantly took the helm and held the boat steady. It was still a pretty perilous operation for Mike as the sea was still heaving and pounding but nonetheless he managed to get my attention and point to the beautiful double rainbow arcing against the pewter sky.

Shortly afterwards we dropped anchor among the lobster pot marker buoys at the entrance to the fishermen's cove in Aberdaron Bay. Mike called Holyhead coastguard on the yacht's radio to say we'd arrived safely. They thanked him for his call but didn't comment on our skills as sailors or even say they were pleased we'd made it. I suppose if they thought anything at all it was just that we were mad to be out there in the first place.

The next morning saw us heading for Bardsey Sound, the treacherous tide race between Bardsey Island and the tip of the Llŷn. Bardsey, Ynys Enlli, is said to be the burial place of 20,000 saints and some people believe it to be the legendary Avalon, where King Arthur died and Merlin the Magician was buried.

Over a beans-on-toast breakfast we discussed our options. Should we try to get through the sound straight away, when the tide was just starting to run against us, or should we leave it until the afternoon when it would be with us? Or should we just stay put until the weather improved? The early morning shipping forecast was again warning of gales in the Irish Sea but, as usual we decided to put our nose out to see what it was like. It looked quite rough from where we were and perhaps we should have heeded the gale warning and stayed put. We were both tired; I had a headache and although the day was reasonably mild and dry it was overcast and very windy.

Of course, once we got going we kept going. Bardsey Sound was its usual inhospitable self and almost before we knew it we were in rip tides in mountainous seas and a good force six or seven to boot. We could hear the wind above the crashing and banging of the boat as she reared up one side of the great rollers only to hurtle down the other. I found it exhilarating and it soon blew away my headache. The waves were huge, powerful, magnificent and breathtakingly beautiful. Because I wasn't helming and didn't have responsibility for the boat it was easy for me just to sit there, enjoy the ride and thrill to the splendour of it all. Above the confused sea and the screaming wind the grey clouds had broken up to reveal an intense blue sky. The sun glinted off the exquisite translucent jade of the waves and spindrift swept across the surface of the water as the yacht's bows forced their way through the surf.

We had just cleared the island and were still battling to get through the last of the overfalls when Cevamp was nearly knocked down by a big wave that caught us broadside on the port beam. It flung me against the lockers and Mike was swept across the cockpit, fighting to retain his hold on the tiller. The foam crashed over the spray-dodgers and right over us before tearing along the length of the boat and ripping one of the starboard stanchion posts from its mounting. Mike was still struggling for control of the boat and shouting at me to put the bloody camera away, grab the bucket and bail. I sheepishly shoved the camera into the pocket of my oilies before dropping onto all fours in the cockpit, bucket and chucking as fast as I could. My efforts had made little difference to the gallons of water sloshing around in the cockpit when we caught another monster, again from the starboard side. I continued bailing until the depth of water diminished to a level that the pump could cope with.

We carried on, slowly easing our way round the tip of the peninsula and away from Bardsey Island, which seemed to be looming behind us for ever. Finally, though, we got through the sound and as the seas were beginning to ease slightly I took over the tiller to give Mike a break. That was when we hit another area of rip tides and from my seat in the cockpit I saw my bag of clothes fly across the cabin to end up floating in the knee-deep water that had forced its way inside.

This time the waves weren't only high but wide too. They loomed vertically ahead of the boat and as usual Cevamp rode decisively up them, balanced for a breathless, motionless moment on the crest then rolled heavily down the other side. Sometimes I thought she'd never make it to the top and would have to go, like Alice, through the glassy green wall, while at other times the waves just broke right over our heads instead. But still my overriding impression was one of indescribable beauty.

Even while all this was going on we could see through the spray to where people were strolling along the cliff path on top of the headland, bright splashes of colour against the green of the fields and the blue sky, and we wondered if they could see how rough it was for us. But it's almost impossible to judge the height and ferocity of waves when you look down on them and although some of the ramblers waved cheerily to us most of them probably never even gave us a second glance.

When we finally reached Porthdinllaen we anchored close to shore, exhausted, cold, wet-booted and soaked to the skin. Our faces and lips were encrusted with dried-on salt, which sparkled in the sun and gave us a slightly frosted appearance. Families were scattered on the beach, eating ice creams and making the most of the glorious weather. They couldn't have known, and wouldn't have cared, about the drama that had been going on just a few miles from where they were enjoying their picnics, playing with their dogs and children, splashing around at the water's edge or simply soaking up the sun. We still couldn't relax though. There was damage to repair and clearing up to do. And most importantly, we needed a cup of tea. We spent the rest of the afternoon mopping up and drying things out and soon the boat resembled a Chinese laundry with trousers flapping from the halyards at the top of the mast and a variety of waterproofs, wellies and spare clothes hanging from the rails.

That evening, lingering over our dinner of beef stew, we talked about our experience.

'Well I don't mind admitting I was frightened,' said Mike, 'especially when those two big waves came over and lifted me up and swamped the cockpit.'

I thought about this for a minute. I wanted to try and be honest with myself. Had I really been as unafraid as I was making out, or was I just trying to make myself out to be cooler than I really was? I've always had this notion that as an Englishwoman I am at my best in times of adversity but was I just kidding myself? Was that coolness just a front, protecting the frightened little girl that I really was? Or had the trials and tribulations of sailing brought out nobler qualities, previously unseen? I was pleased with my decision.

'I may have been a bit anxious,' I told Mike, 'but I really wasn't that scared. Probably because I trust you and know you know what you're doing, and I truly believed Cevamp would cope. But if I'd been on my own or in charge of the boat for some other reason, say if you'd been knocked unconscious by the boom, I think I would have been terrified.'

I chewed thoughtfully on a gravy-enriched dumpling. 'Mind you,' I added, 'I'm not saying that I'd particularly choose to do it again!'

In the end we agreed we had been foolhardy to put to sea in the first place that day, especially having heard the gale warnings. Cevamp had taken a real pounding and we made a decision that in future, out of respect for the boat if nothing else, we would always stay in harbour if the forecast predicted anything above a force six. We paid close attention to the early evening shipping forecast.

After that, the weather took pity on us and we awoke to one of those perfect days that make you realise why you go sailing. During the afternoon, just when we thought the day couldn't get better, we spotted a pod of seven bottle-nosed dolphins, including two mothers and babies. They were quite a long way off but as we watched we realised they had seen us and were deliberately coming our way, arching out of the water with a casual fluidity that belied their speed.

They stayed with us for an hour and were so close that they made Cevamp's echo sounder bleep as they leapt and dived around us, flashing first out of the water then swooping smoothly under the boat, to reappear just ahead, beside or behind us. We could easily see individual markings and scars on their silvery bodies and were soon able to pick out one from another – one, with a ragged dorsal fin, was especially distinctive. It seemed to us, watching spellbound from the cockpit, that the biggest animal, almost slate-grey in colour, was not only leader but also senior choreographer.

I've read there is believed to be a special kind of symbiosis between dolphins and humans, that there is even some kind of telepathic communication between the species, and it certainly felt like it to Mike and me that day. We sensed strongly that the dolphins were putting on a show especially for us. Their strength and power is hugely impressive, yet they are so graceful and friendly, smiling all the time and always making eye contact, as if seeking our friendship and approval. The mothers and their enchanting babies moved me to tears as they breached and dived, always perfectly synchronised and always with their pectoral flippers touching, just as a human mother and toddler hold hands on a shopping trip. We couldn't take our eyes off them.

All of a sudden the mood changed. As one, they became very excited. The pace of the display quickened from relaxed to frenzied and they transmitted their excitement to us. It was a strong group feeling and we were part of it.

'Perhaps they're planning something special for us,' I said.

We watched, mesmerised, as, with perfect timing, they leapt towards, over and under each other, always conscious of the speed and position of the boat and always just slightly ahead. Then, just as suddenly, they all calmed down. All, that is, except the big leader. He began to thrash violently around, his entire body twisting out of the water in a series of massive horizontal body flips and ending each move with a thrust of his tail, before crashing back under the surface.

Then came the finale. We could scarcely contain ourselves.

'What's he doing? What's he doing?' was all I could say and Mike was breathing 'Magic, magic,' over and over again as the big dark leader rose beak first, vertically out of the water, just yards from our starboard bow. We were both holding our breath.

He rose up, up and up until he was about a metre clear of the water. He gave a thrash of his tail and then flung himself sideways. There was a thundering crash that vibrated through the hull of the boat as he threw himself back into the sea. He gave a repeat performance and a final encore.

Suddenly they were all gone. The water was still again. It was as though they'd never been there.

Tears were streaming down our cheeks. It was such an emotional performance and we had to remind ourselves that these were wild animals. They hadn't been trained in some obscene dolphinarium, or bribed with fish to perform to order. They were happy, in their own element and dancing for the sheer joy of it. Dancing for us.

With the disappearance of the dolphins and the smoothing of the sea, it was back to the business of sailing for Mike and me and we returned to our seats in the cockpit. But something had changed for us both that afternoon. We'd never previously taken for granted our good fortune in having a yacht to sail but now we felt immensely privileged to have witnessed such an enchanting celebration of the sheer joy of being alive. Sitting there, surrounded by the beauty of the scenery on land and the awesome power of the sea around our little boat, all thoughts of our storm-tossed couple of days had flown. This was where I wanted to be.

Cwm Idwal

❧

Jean Lyon

The journey to Cwm Idwal began decades ago. Perhaps it started in my childhood in the flat mid-lands of England when, as a wild, untidy girl, I challenged the Gods that I could take the valleys of despair if only I could have the peaks, the glorious peaks of existence. I sought out mountains in Scotland and found vastness and a strange sense of peace: to be away from all of man's fallible structures. I walked through the Canadian Rockies and was afraid of the true wilderness, attracted by paths not made by man, but afraid of what I might encounter. And then I travelled to North Wales and found the mountains where I belong, the mountains that frame my days, always before my wide open eyes or glimpsed above the trees, or below me when I glide through them in my dreams.

We discovered Cwm Idwal late on a day spent walking from Capel Curig on the old drovers' road. We arrived at the hostel as planned and, unburdened by rucksacks, sat in the sun and looked up at the path towards Pen-yr-Ole Wen. We planned to walk back to Rowen along the top of the Carneddau, and the map showed that this was the way. It looked impossible, sheer from the A5 and barely marked. Discouraged, we turned away and wandered down beside the river, finding with delight the waterfall, hidden from the road. We washed our well-used feet and balanced on the wet rocks, contentedly looking for fish or eels. But the day was not done. Turning back to the hostel, another path, unchecked on the map, unplanned, called us away.

We walked on a rising path to a mountain gate and across a bridge. Except that we did not cross, but stood transfixed by the river that roared towards us and dropped under our feet, pouring on towards the waterfall, the Ffrancon valley, Bethesda, under the new motorway and out into the Straits by Penrhyn Castle. Here it is wild, off the mountain, collecting strength from a shoal of streams, full of life; at the Straits it is constrained by the sludge of the mud banks of Traeth Lafan as it pushes forward to meet the sea.

We walked on, up a rough broad path, highland pasture on either side, the smell of sheep in the air, towards a range of mountains. Nothing prepared us for Llyn Idwal. The flanks of the Glyders were visible from the beginning, but we were almost at the next gate when the lake appeared before us. Had we read the map we would have known, but I am grateful for that moment, surprised by the wild beauty of the cwm, encircled by cliffs of granite, seeming to rise straight up from the water. I take my special visitors there, trying to re-create for them that moment; again and again it happens for me, or is it the memory of the first time that I re-remember?

We walked along the path ascending on the eastern side of Llyn Idwal, beneath the Slabs which still held climbers spidering upwards and across its flats, and beyond to where the path became steep, and then a scramble, clambering like a child on all fours, excited by the adventure. We didn't know that we were under the Devil's Kitchen, Twll Du, where the Snowdon Lily hides itself on high clefts and blooms in secret. We did know that we could see the Straits and Ynys Môn beyond, and we could just see the hills they call Holyhead Mountain.

That day, we went on, up the penance of a scree slope to Glyder Fawr, across the moonscape of Castell-y-Gwynt and on to Glyder Fach before descending by what I now know is the Miners' path. We did not find the cantilever rock, because we did not know to look for it. We came to the saddle that separates Tryfan from the Glyders. Tryfan of the Adam and Eve rock towers, Tryfan of the Heather Terrace and paths which disappear before walls of rock, Tryfan the guardian of the Nant Ffrancon. We did not wash our feet in Llyn Bochlwyd beneath Tryfan: the day was losing light and we could see a downward scramble ahead. We were back at the hostel before darkness and the rain arrived.

❦

On other days I have encircled the lake, choosing to turn west after the climb instead of continuing to the peaks. There is an overhanging rock that would make a shelter, I like to think, if I were a bear or a mountain lion. Better still, there is a boulder, just off the path, that makes a very suitable perch for contemplation. The way down becomes unclear, a choice of narrow ridges of wet slate and streaming slabs. But I feel safe when I can hold onto the rock, search for my next move, grope for my next handhold; I have only once felt the panic that turned my legs to water, and that was on a steep grassy slope above the sea. Too soon, the excitement turns to relief as I find the gritted, paved path on the western bank. Sometimes, when the climb seems too daunting, I slip down beneath the slabs and cross the squelching sphagnum moss at the head of the lake, and find a way back up to that far pavement. It leads round slowly to a sandy beach. Once I even swam in the shallows from that sandy beach, but the weather was particularly hot that summer. More often, I have sat on the sand and looked across to the mountain skyline and seen birds on display, or watched sheep follow one another up inaccessible slopes. I have sat upon a rock above the lake and stared into its dark waters and seen no bottom. There must be fish, but I have seen no fish. The sheep were probably bleating; sheep usually do. And the birds were probably calling. But I remember the sloughing of the wind and the splashing of water and a strange quietness that flowed between. And I was disappearing; I was part of the rock, of the lake, of the cwm.

I do not need to know that geologically this is a remarkable place, that the lake lies in the hollow that once contained a glacier which scraped out the valley beneath. I do not need to learn the names of all the plants that grow within this Nature Reserve. I hear the wind that scours the cwm, I see the petrol colours in the wet rock below Twll Du, I feel my pulse quicken as I approach the raging stream above the slabs and dare myself to leap across, or pole my way through icy waters if I feel less brave. On days of cold and rain, I do not choose to visit Cwm Idwal, but I have been caught there when the weather turns. It is still a joy, if there can be joy when you suffer the misery of wet trousers where the rain has dripped from your coat, and rain that stings your face and no choice but to bend into the wind and walk. It feels like survival, and you are surviving and small things, small niggles, have no place in your struggle.

We did not climb the disappearing path up Pen-yr-Ole Wen, at least not on that first occasion. A mountain rescue alarm and inclement weather seemed like warnings from above. Instead, we took the less arduous route, down the valley to Bethesda and along the coast back to the Conwy valley. I climbed it later, in my fiftieth year, when I climbed all fourteen peaks of Yr Eyri, not as a marathon, but as more modest ridge walks, with experienced walkers to show me the way. We climbed up to the top of the Carneddau, we walked down the length of the Glyders and down the ridge on the northern side of the Ogwen Valley. We climbed Tryfan (but did not jump from Adam to Eve) and we climbed up and round the Snowdon Horseshoe. I wept with exhaustion when I had to climb over the hydro-pipe at the end of the walk.

I love the names of the peaks on which I have rested, the lesser ones and of the greater. I learned them all. How glad I am that this is so, now that I no longer climb. I drive through the valleys, I walk in the valleys, and I call to them all silently, by name, to tell them I am here.

A Horizontal View

✣

Patricia Barrie

The nineteen fifties were early days both for the NHS and for antibiotics, and the adults were still marvelling about them when I took sick and needed both. My father sat me down, tapped the box in which the miracle drug was housed and announced gravely, 'This is worth more than the average weekly wage and you'll need a box every month for many months to come. If it were not for the NHS I could not afford it. You would die.'

I had already lost my mother, both maternal grandparents and my paternal grandfather, so I should have had a pretty clear idea of death in all its varieties. But I was nine years old and thus immortal. Death was for others, not for me.

'So I hope you'll appreciate it,' my father continued, 'and take every dose with gratitude.' I have a vague recollection of his adding, '— as a duty to the nation,' but I can't now be sure; it was too long ago.

I did not feel ill, just tired; so that when I was put to bed in the best back bedroom, propped comfortably against a heap of pillows, I felt fine again and, soon after that, bored stiff. I read a little, slept a little, woke up and gazed at the view.

We lived at the inland edge of a seaside town in South Wales, far enough from the sea to forget all about it except on dim winter nights, when we heard the foghorn bawling like a cow for its calf. Cows and calves were in fact more my scene. The view from the back bedroom was of fields and a farmyard, where the cows came and went twice a day, even in November, and the gateways where they waited for their call to milking were a sludge of oily green that looked colder, far colder, than snow.

It was a horizontal view. The hedge at the bottom of our garden sat as if on the windowsill, and the hedge beyond that - in reality about a hundred yards distant - just another inch higher up. There were three fields altogether, with four hedges to divide them, and then the glorious Great Meadow, like a vast green velvet cushion, with a group of elm trees near its bottom edge of which I became very fond. They were like a family: three big ones, three little. Even as a child, my imagination did not tend towards the soppy: they were never 'Mummy Elm and Baby Elm, Daddy, Granny and the twins.' As fond as I was of them, they were just trees. Suspended from the biggest was a tractor tyre where, in summer, children could swing. I had never swung there, although in the months that followed my heart yearned towards that tractor tyre as it has rarely, since, yearned towards anything else. To a child of nine, a tyre suspended from a tree is a vision of heaven.

The liveliest corner of my view was the farmyard, a tumbled geometry of brick and stone and galvanised iron. The farmer and his boy were made tiny by distance and it was hard at first to distinguish one from the other. But it was the boy who came to fetch the cows and I learned him like a line of poetry: the way he walked, the way he turned his head, the way he unlatched a five-bar gate and stood on the bottom rung to ride it as it opened. Sometimes he looked up at my window and waved, making a long day shorter. Like most little girls, I disliked little boys, but he was twelve, which was perfect.

The farmhouse was very ancient and although from my point of view it looked like a child's drawing of a house - door in the middle, two windows either side - it was at least four rooms deep and provided all kinds of 'offices' on the farmyard side. It had mains drainage and running water but no gas or electricity. In winter the farmer's family cooked on a coal range and in summer on an oil stove, but at night they managed with candles and hurricane lamps and I caught scarcely a glimmer of these when darkness fell.

My miracle medicine was a gritty white powder in a paper sachet. 'Mix with milk,' it advised, although this was easier said than done. Whizz it with a teaspoon all you liked, the grit still ended up, all by itself, at the bottom of the glass. It tasted foul. My father stood over me for the first few weeks, making me swallow every grain. But then he sent my sister to do the evil deed and she only said, 'Medicine,' before handing me the glass and marching out again, job done. There was a rainwater tank on the wall outside the window, and it performed my 'duty to the nation' with admirable fortitude. The rainwater soon turned milky and, fearing discovery, I created a diversion when anyone went too near the window. I also feared the roses would die when my father watered them the following summer. But they lived and, more by luck than good judgement, so did I.

Before the advent of antibiotics, tuberculosis had been a killer and largely incurable, although the disease could be contained by long months of bed-rest. The idea was that the infected patch of lung could be sealed off by scar tissue – the scar forming only when the patient's breathing was minimised. You just lay there, in short, barely moving, allowing the lung to rest and the infection to be bricked up, like a naughty nun in a convent wall. Bed-rest was not strictly necessary once the drugs became available, but the doctors dared not believe this at first and they cured you both ways. It was just as well in my case. Not only did I give half my medicine to the roses, I also spent half my time turning somersaults in bed.

The disease was infectious and I was not allowed visitors from school. Even the adults spent no more time than was necessary in my company. My thirteen year old sister was permitted to walk in, say hello and walk out again, but neither of us would have wanted more; a four year gap between sisters is like the no-man's land between armies: one side or the other might take a step forward, but only to shout 'yah-sucks,' across the gap.

My grandmother cooked and delivered my meals and afterwards collected the tray, usually bringing a duster in her apron pocket so that her ten minutes of keeping me company need not be deemed a waste of time. It was a year after the end of food rationing - a fifteen year stint of rationing that had marked every woman's mind and made food a sacred matter. 'There's an egg in it,' Gran would say, in hushed, respectful tones. Or, 'Eat it all up; there's best butter on it.' The day the farmer brought me a handful of ducks' eggs was a day of celebration. '*Fresh–laid* eggs, full of goodness,' my grandmother announced, with awe. 'I'll make you a nice omelette. Do you the world of good.'

The farmer's gift made me feel very honoured, although he was not allowed to come and see me. Afterwards, I looked for him to wave my thanks, but there was no one about. I hadn't even seen the boy since Christmas.

I had plenty of time to study the landscape, to watch how it changed, turning silver in hoar frosts and white in the snow. My window faced west and I enjoyed the sunsets, although the time I liked best was when the sun had gone and lilac-coloured clouds sat on the horizon in such a way that you would swear they were mountains. The first time this happened I was shocked at my own ignorance: 'I didn't know there were mountains here!' But they faded into darkness and, next morning, were gone.

It snowed more than once, making me ache to play

snowballs and mourn my lost hope when the thaw came. The land is never darker than it is after snow. Maybe it's just the contrast between cold purity and muddy thaw, or perhaps snow deals death to a few green things that were alive before the blizzard. Whatever the reasons, my view was a cheerless one through much of January and I read all the books I could lay hands on until the sun shone again.

The public library allowed me two books a week. My sister borrowed another two and my grandmother two more. I read them all and in desperation attempted my father's tomes on anthropology and science. Gran enjoyed a good cowboy story. She had little patience with romance (which I'd have preferred) and was tired of the classics, which dwelt behind glass in my grandfather's bookcase, downstairs.

'Nothing to read,' was my moan when Gran asked how I was. 'Nothing to read, nothing to *read*.'

For a while she refused to open the bookcase, deeming me too young for Charles Dickens and George Eliot, but eventually she relented and, when the novels failed to stop me, she brought poetry: Longfellow, Keats and Francis Thompson. I read them all, although I understood very little and afterwards forgot them, except for Longfellow's *Wreck of the Hesperus*, which I learned by heart and can still quote at length. The bookcase also offered up the *Complete Illustrated Household Encyclopaedia*, which taught me, on just one of its thousand pages, how to make doughnuts, to keep doves, make dovetail joints, play draughts and make a draining rack for teacups.

It eventually dawned on me that the best hope I had of reading *my* sort of literature (about nine-year old girls who have their own ponies) was to write it myself. This I did and afterwards was much happier. The same has been true ever since: not that I continue to write about girls and their ponies, but that I'm happiest when writing. It can probably be said that my illness was a gift to demonstrate a gift I already possessed.

On a day near the end of February I looked from my window and found that winter had stripped the land to a skeleton between whose bones I could see things I'd never seen before: the topmost stones of the thirteenth century church, the outline of the water tower at the top of Wenvoe Lane and, more thrilling yet, a chimney poking through the trees in the woods beyond Great Meadow. The woods were further away than they seemed – a mile or so as the crow flies, maybe two miles by the lanes. I had never been there and had no idea who could live, so secretly, in the woods. Gran had never heard of a house there. Neither had my father. The mystery became a work for my imagination and a goal – like the tyre in the elm tree – labelled, 'When I Am Well Again'.

I was allowed to get up by easy stages: an hour after lunch, then (three weeks later) another hour after tea. By half-hour increments these two separate hours nudged closer together until I was up for four hours, then six. Before my tenth birthday, in April, I was well enough for a walk around the block. Away from my window everything was strange. The front of the house was an alien place where people walked and children played. There were lamp posts, an occasional motor car and a great many straight lines: kerbs, walls, windows and, on the corner, a big red telephone box.

I did not belong at the front of the house and had no desire to remain there, but it was May before I managed a walk to the farm. It was like walking into a picture, leaving the confines of the picture frame behind. Like all things in life, however, the reality did not match the dream. As I arrived in the farmyard the boy sped away from it on his bike, shouting hello in friendly enough fashion, but leaving me behind. I asked the farmer if I could swing on the tyre in Great Meadow and he said, 'Wait until the hay's in, next month.'

No one in those days worried over-much about children's safety. Once they could walk and talk, cross the road by the preferred method and keep their balance on a bike, they were simply turned out of doors with instructions to be home in time for tea. It was like this when I decided to find the house in the woods; no thought of danger crossed Gran's mind. Just, 'Take it slowly and if you feel yourself tiring, come straight home.' I, of course, thought of dangers galore: Hansel and Gretel and the wicked witch in her gingerbread house; Snow White and her evil stepmother; Red Riding Hood and the wolf. But I was excited, not afraid. Seeking that house in the woods was like turning a page to find an answer, a story's end.

I took my walk slowly, as Gran had advised, but did not tire until I was too far from home to make a return possible. I was nearing my target and kept going, hoping that a kind lady, rather than a wicked witch, might offer lemonade when I arrived. But the kind lady (like the boy) had found somewhere else to go and her house was abandoned, shuttered and barred. Its most welcoming feature was a verandah overlooking an overgrown garden, where orchard trees and old roses competed for space with an invading force of brambles. I sat and rested, daydreamed and perhaps slept. I have no recollection of being joined by someone else. All I remember is that he said, 'If we sit very quietly the animals will come.'

So we sat there, very quietly, and I noticed that he was dark, his clothes tattered, his skin ingrained with dirt. I can still see him in my mind's eye and guess now that he was about forty. I guess also that he was a remnant of the war: a man who came home – maybe late, from the Far East – to find his home bombed or his wife gone. There were enough men like him to make the type recognisable, even to me. He was a tramp, a vagrant. He didn't say so, but I think it more than likely that I, in sitting on that verandah, had invaded his bedroom.

The animals came: first a cock pheasant, then a dozen or so rabbits, all of which disappeared on the entrance of a stoat and its brood: a demonic troupe of tiny athletes that danced like sunbeams, chasing each other through the garden faster than thought. I wanted to laugh, but held my breath, wishing it could last forever. In all of my months of watching, I had seen nothing like it. Like the last brushstrokes of a painting, it finished my landscape and made it complete.

He said he would walk home with me. I had told him that I'd been ill, that this was my first long walk, my big adventure, and I think he might have worried I would collapse on the way home. It was getting late. Neither of us had a watch, but I was beginning to think teatime might have come and gone without me.

My escort crossed the road just before we reached home and sped away on the opposite pavement, as my father, his face a shade paler than usual, met me at the gate.

'Who was *that*?'

'I don't know; I met him in the woods; he was nice.'

My father was silent. Later, when I was on my way (quite gratefully) to bed, he said, 'Try to choose your friends more carefully. People are not always as nice as they seem. Your tramp might have been dangerous.'

I smiled. 'But he wasn't.'

In June, I helped bring in the hay and afterwards spent an entire afternoon swinging on the tyre in the elm tree. Three years later they chopped down all the elms – parents and baby, granny and the twins – and built bungalows in their place. Beloved corners remained until I went away to college, but the whole landscape has gone now and there are blocks of flats where the woods used to be.

Throwing the Magnet

❧

Jay Griffiths

Nature doesn't often make me elegiac. Not when I'm in it. It makes me Anglo-Saxon, it makes me laugh, it makes me wiggle, it makes me six.

You see, I like bashing frozen puddles and putting icicles in my mouth. I like getting to the tops of mountains. Fast. The impish whistles ping louder than the wind murmurs in its evocations. Later the elegy. Now, the now alone, wet, free, tenseless.

Sometimes, I get a sneaky feeling that nature doesn't much like being written down. I think she prefers songlines and stories of land-aloud, or tuneless hums on the way. I think she'd rather have the tale of paths told by the feet. A leaf-pile kicked up into the air, not a library, locked in shelves. So liberate the books and let the land talk.

Here it speaks of deft and soft-handed care, a coppice knitted gentle by the way, a quilted field or two. There,

three oak trees stand so very close, making a circle big
enough for three to kiss. The Afon Marteg is fishing and
has caught a tired salmon, snagged a rock, poached a
pool and from a high ledge, fly-fishing forever, it casts a
graceful waterfall.

In the small town where I live, musicians play every
week in the pub; the harpist with luminous eyes, a quiet
man until his fingers sing. For me, their music carries to the
hills; they fiddle up the valleys, they flute the wind on the
mountain tops. This valley is a place of rainbows, elusive,
eldritch hints. It used to be known for *dweomercræft*; the
craft of healers, magicians, those who know spells, those
who know the sourcery of words. Of course. It is a land
where all the streams are young: unmemoried water which
carries no past of courses gone by. Of course they laugh,
of course they heal, the sources of Wye and Severn and
Clywedog.

These hills are tender to this town, and the rivers
generous. There is happiness in the valleysides. Me, I'm
old enough to have scars on my soul but young enough to
be still surprised by the permanence of grief, how it goes
quiet but never leaves.

I used to live here, in this town right in the heart of
Wales. I moved away. I have just returned. My grandfather
was Welsh. He moved away. I have returned to his land.
Why has this place given me so sweet a welcome? I'm
only a bit Welsh, I don't speak the language. But I feel
well-come, here, in this rugged, cosy land, with its curly
surprises. (Ieuan, the day before he dies, weaving up Great

Oak Street, high on morphine to control the pain from the cancer which will get him tomorrow, has Johnny Cash at full volume, blaring out of the speakers on his scooter, when his mobile phone goes off with the ringtone of Old Macdonald had a Farm.)

The one good thing about not knowing Welsh is that at every turn I'm reminded that there are layers on layers of land I do not know. I cannot pretend to the glib understanding I could feel in Somerset or Staffordshire. Like most blow-ins, the first language I learnt was traffic signs. Araf. Dim parcio. But as I walk these hills, I've tried to familiarize myself with all the river names. Afon Clywedog 'heard from afar'. Nant Cynnydd, 'stream of growth, increase' (with overtones of that lovely Anglo-Saxon word cunt, to English ears). Nant Gwyllt, 'wild stream'. Nant y Bradnant, 'stream of the treacherous valley'. It is treacherously steep. But *brad* means treachery or conspiracy and conspiracy recalls co-inspiring; a word with many harmonies. So the stream of co-inspiring is my loose translation, for myself. It seems appropriate to learn a little language from rivers. Rivers and languages are similar, after all, they spring from sources deep underground. They are both living, moving things and you never step into the same language twice. Large rivers, opening out to the seas, can be grandly silent – old, quiet, no need for chatter. Here, the rivers are young and talkative; the streams lean their elbows on the banksides and gossip with the neighbours; there is a chat-up line in every waterfall. This land has a knack for story telling.

My friend has been very ill. His lips were grey, his skin was blue-grey and yellow. When this illness first hit him, he couldn't breathe, his chest hurt, and he had thought he was dying. You can't die, it's rude. At least you can't die without doing your utmost to avoid it. So we walked every day, through every weather, for hours and hours. There is medicine in these hills, and we found it, tramping for days in dogged pursuit of health. This is lucky land. Not for the farmers, no, not at this moment in history, but in the long run, this land is healthy, vital and kind as wool. Unpretentious, open-hearted country.

A few days ago we walked past a holiday house. It was *tastefully* done up. Renovated *beautifully*. No expense spared. It was ship-shape and well-furnished but entirely empty of ornery stuff. No day-to-day living was going on, and it made me sick. There are people who can't afford a home, but here, someone has a house just for a toy. In the kindness of this land, this house jars. It mocks the principle of hearth. It is an act of cruelty. Too many people's lives have been deformed by not having a home. Too many people have had their spirits eroded by the rootlessness of housing poverty. It's a weird, modern version of the clearances: I have too many friends who have had to emigrate because they can't afford a home in their own country. Driven out by people who buy houses as if they were playing Monopoly.

The owners doubtless think they own this place. I don't. Nothing is owned by buying. You own things by dwelling in them, with them, by knowing things, by loving them.

❦

On Christmas Day, we climbed Fan hill, myself, my fast-recovering poet-friend and another friend, a saxophonist. All of us have some deeply scorched paths of memory. All of us know a loss of hope, for lover, child and dream. Between us we have lost to death two parents and a partner, lost a home of forty years and two beloved friends gone. All of us know the sound of the heart breaking. But all of us have also known the heartmending on hillsides and at the hearthsides of friends. We lit a candle and tucked it behind stones and moss. We flew a kite in high, cold sky. We drank homemade damson gin and laughed a lot. Earth, air, fire and water. The elements of the heart. Shall we go home? This is one. But we do turn down at twilight, to friends and a fire.

The year is turning – very old and very young. Christmas has just dusked and New Year is lighting the way ahead. These winter twilights, you can feel the gloaming moment on your skin, the sun in the afternoon wrapped up in midnight blue and put down. The crib of the day, the crib of the year. We are far from summer now. Each evening is a nostalgia, turn for home, fold into pubs and friends and slippers. It is a time of hearths. Hearth, that beautiful word which is itself a home to so many words of home: heart, earth, eat, tea, heat.

This is a land which is very old and very young. Geologically, one of the oldest places in Britain. The rocks here are older than almost any. But the rivers are so young and they scamper like children in wellies, splashing across a bog, springs welling up in the land like the laughter welling up in the child. I like old things: old friends, old clothes, old trees, old language, old people, old jokes. The glinting is on them. I like young things, too, a tree cub and a sapling child. Sometimes I just don't particularly like things in between, too busy, too literal and unlustrous. My love for this land is sapling now, curious, uninformed, hopeful, green. And I hope it will grow old here, creased, unsurprisable, golden. Right now, I'm a stranger on the cusp of belonging, knocking a bit tentatively at the don't-yet-know. To dwell is to know, to know is to belong, to belong is to love. The heart is simple.

It began with one stone by one streamside, one green and shimmering afternoon, several years ago. I was walking with a copy of John Clare's poems and found a smooth black stone tucked against a tree trunk, so I could sit on it, with my feet in the stream and my back against the alder. I kept a tryst there with John Clare. If he'd come across the idea of holiday-homes, that nasty self-contradiction, he would have gone for walks with matches in his pocket.

I've returned to that stone again and again, poem-stone, kissing-stone, swimming-stone. I like returns. The heart returns to what it has loved. Nostalgia. Hiraeth. Turn and return in the pathways of the mind, tracks of memory, those pathways which deepen with each tread of thought. The mind has holloways, the trodden ways, felted with leaves, the hedgen keeping steppage with the paths, tree roots above you. The paths are founded by first choosing but profounded by return.

Like Don Quixote, I have thrown the magnet of my motion ahead of me. On two levels. I choose, this day, this path, on an OS map, the scale is 1:25,000. The other scale is one to lifesize; how I choose to walk the paths of the days of this my life.

On New Year's Eve, we climbed the same hill, the same two friends and I. This time, we climbed at midnight, following a path we knew well. We saw two hares boxing at the bottom of the hill, and at the top we flew ribbons of prayer flags and drank two tiny bottles of fizzy wine. We threw six bright stones to the winds, 'for absent friends and lost friends' said the poet whose voice cracked with the weight of six past tenses. And the saxophonist played a deep blue solo to the darkness of the night until the midnight of the day and of the year chimed with a madeleine of all rivermusic; a stream of bells was ringing, almost inaudible from three miles away, the bells of the church of Saint Idloes, which rose with the saxophone and the prayer flags and the love of auld acquaintance, old friends and old land, into air and memory.

Author Biographies

Sue Anderson lives in Monmouth with her husband and two cats. She spent a lot of time teaching teenagers, but is now trying to give it up. She has had short stories, poetry, and a few articles published. In 2005 she won the British Fantasy Society short story competition. Her ambition is to publish a novel - she has written several, and one received a bursary from the Welsh Arts Council.

Patricia Barrie was born and educated in Wales but now lives with her husband in a village near Bath. Her first novel, *Devotions*, was published by Chatto & Windus in 1986 and she has written two further novels, *Rosie* (Hamish Hamilton,1988) and *Songs of Silence* (Honno 1999), plus numerous pieces for a variety of magazines. She has also written four novels under the pseudonym Anna Barrie.

Sarah Jane Boss was born and raised in Bristol, where she was able to pick up Welsh radio. From an early age she had a liking for Welsh language and folk music, and the stories of the *Mabinogion*. She is now a lecturer in Christian theology at the University of Wales, Lampeter, where she specialises in the theology and cult of the Virgin Mary, and the theology of creation in relation to ecology.

Paula Brackston's first book was an account of her horseback trek around Wales *–The Dragon's Trail*. She lives in the Brecon Beacons with her partner and two children. She has an MA in Creative Writing and works part-time as a script reader. Paula produces short stories for magazines and is currently working on a novel. She was recently shortlisted in the Crème de la Crime Search. She also runs creative writing classes locally.

Maggie Cainen loves living by the sea in Swansea. Educated Manchester, London and Swansea Universities. MA: Creative Writing and Media Studies 2004. Former modern languages teacher, water sports instructor and avid participant in most adrenaline sports. She is a regular writer for scuba magazines *Diver* and *Dive*. She is a wide reader, with a huge field of interests. She is a short story and children's writer, especially teenage novels.

Katherine Cuthbert lives in south Cheshire. Besides her contribution to *In Her Element* she has written other pieces about handcycling for various disability and cycling publications. She has also written about riding her tricycle and tandem tricycle (with husband Pete). Currently she is working on completing a memoir commenting on life coping with MS. The memoir is titled *Keeping Balance: a psychologist's experience of coping with chronic illness and disability.*

Siân Melangell Dafydd was bought up at the foot of

the Berwyn. Her work includes poetry, prose and essays for *Planet, New Welsh Review, Taliesin* and *Tu Chwith*. She has contributed to *Laughing not Laughing* (Honno), *Straeon y Troad* (Gomer) , *Hon: Ynys y Galon* (Gomer) and *Coming up Roses* (Honno).

Jackie Davies, originally from Sussex, spent her childhood painting and writing stories and fell in love with Wales at the age of twelve. She moved to Denbigh in 1994 and spent six years in the Tanat valley before settling in Bala in 2007. She enjoys sketching Welsh mountains and farmhouses, has written articles on language learning and emotional healing and published her first novel, *About Elin*, with Honno in 2007.

Christine Evans has published seven collections of poetry. *Selected Poems* won the inaugural Roland Mathias Prize in 2005 and *Growth Rings* (Seren) was shortlisted for the 2007 Wales Book of the Year. Her latest book is *Burning the Candle* (Gomer), a single long poem and journal about writing it. Her personal history of Bardsey with photo-essays by Wolf Marloh, is published by Gomer in 2008.

Gwyneth Evans grew up and worked on the family farm on the rugged Pembrokeshire coast near to Strumble Head. After moving to Fishguard she worked as a carer. After early retirement, and encouraged by membership of a local writers group, she began to record some of her experiences. Gwyneth also enjoys writing stories based on legends and folk tales of the area. This is her first publishing success.

Jay Griffiths is the award-winning author of *Wild: An Elemental Journey* and *Pip Pip: A Sideways Look at Time*. She won the Discover Award for the best new non-fiction writer in the USA. Her work has appeard in various publications including the *London Review of Books*, the *Idler*, *Ecologist*, *Resurgence*, the *Observer* and the *Guardian*.

Emily Hinshelwood – a self-confessed novice when it comes to wildlife. She upshifted from London ten years ago to a small village at the foot of the Black Mountain where she now writes poetry and plays. Interacting with the landscape has an impact on the way she approaches her writing: walking along the cusp of sea and land has made her strive for a combination of fluidity and solidity which seems to reflect so many aspects of life.

Barbara Jones has had a lifelong interest in many aspects of mountains, including their ecology, geomorphology and vegetation and has spent many a happy hour exploring, climbing and walking in Snowdonia and in other mountain ranges of the world. Since 1985 she has worked in conservation and is currently the Countryside Council for Wales' Upland Ecologist. Her research into the ecology, genetics and conservation of the Snowdon Lily further developed her interest and specialism in arctic-alpine flora.

Ruth Joseph freelanced for IPC magazines. *The Complete Dieter* was commissioned by WH Smith. *Red Stilettos* was published after gaining an M.Phil in Writing, from Glamorgan University. Then her memoir, *Remembering Judith* described caring for her anorexic mother. She is a Rhys Davies Prize winner, won the Litchfield Short Story Prize, published in anthologies including Honno, Parthian, *New Welsh Review*, *Loki*, the *Guardian*, *Red* magazine and has a column in *W* magazine.

Hilary Lloyd, a former nursery nurse, teacher and farmer, lived and worked in the Welsh Marches for twenty-five years. She has had short stories published and her first novel, *A Necessary Killing*, was published last year. She is now concentrating on promoting her book and on her favourite writing medium – short stories. Her dream is to have a collection published, and read.

Jean Lyon lives in an old house near Bangor, North Wales. Her research into the bilingual language development of children on Ynys Môn resulted in a book, *Becoming Bilingual*, published by Multilingual Matters in 1996. In her writing she looks to communication and misunderstanding between people as they try to make sense of their lives against the backcloth of the natural world. She is currently editing her first novel.

Jane Matthews was born in Bristol in 1972, studied Fine Art at Oxford University and Art History at The

Courtauld Institute in London. She lived on Skomer Island between 2003 and 2007 with Juan - the Warden, their daughter Martha and about half a million seabirds. Jane studied the grey seal breeding season as part of a long-term monitoring programme, writing and painting in her spare time. Her book, *Skomer, Portrait of a Welsh Island* was published by Graffeg in 2007.

Dee Rivaz was born in Cumbria in 1953, and now lives in Denbighshire. Her research has been aknowledged in *Too Much Too Young*, about growing up in the 80's, Pan 1981, and she is co-author of *Brickworks*, a literacy resource published by LDA 1998. She began freelancing as a writer in 2006 and set up the Pinboard Writing Workshops. She is currently working on a collection of poetry and a biography.

Carys Shannon grew up on the beautiful Gower peninsular and is currently based in Swansea. After studying Theatre at the University of Wales, Aberystwyth she has worked in the performing arts for the last four years. This is her first published piece of writing and she would like to dedicate it to the memory of her mother, Angela. Carys is currently working on a full length novel.

Martha Stephens lives in Blaenavon in South Wales. Her short stories have been published in several anthologies including *Broken Hearts* - a collection of stories of domestic violence. Her article on gold panning in North Wales was published in October 2007. After two years of research, she is nearing completion of her book about the children who worked in the pits and mines of Wales.

Jill Teague was born in the Rhondda Valley and studied English Literature at Swansea University and subsequently taught English for 25 years. She is currently studying to be a Certified Poetry Therapy Practitioner with Bridgexngs Poetry Center, NYC. Jill was awarded a grant by the center in 2006 to develop her 'Treading Softly – Writing in Nature' work with oncology patients. In 2007 she also received a research grant from Wales Arts International in relation to this work.

Elaine Walker writes fiction, non-fiction and poetry from her home on the Denbigh Moors. She has work published in the UK and USA and her first book, *Horse*, is forthcoming from Reaktion Books as part of their series on animals in cultural history. Elaine teaches creative writing in university and community classes as well as one-to-one and is on Academi's list of mentors.

Jackie Willamson has been a compulsive scribbler since she first learnt to hold a pencil. A career in journalism and PR in the Home Counties was followed by early retirement to Pembrokeshire, where she takes inspiration from her surroundings while out walking the coast path with her husband and two beagles. A founder member of Fishguard Acorns Writers' Group, Jackie published her first book, *Cevamp, Mike and Me*, in 2007.

Editor's biography

Jane MacNamee is a nature and travel writer devoting most of her work to the British landscape. Her writing and book reviews have appeared in *BBC History* magazine, *Time Out*, *Resurgence*, *Pure-Organic Living Magazine*, *Gwales*, a number of poetry magazines, *This Mountain* (Gomer) and The Rough Guide series. She has been living and walking in the mountains of Wales for twelve years, with a two year interlude working at Schumacher College in Devon. She is currently working on her own collection of essays about our changing relationship to the natural world.

Other titles from Honno

Even the Rain is Different
Edited by Gwyneth Tyson Roberts

From sleeping in trees in Corsica to escaping Stalinist purges in Moscow. From Southern Europe to South America, Russia to Australia. Welsh Women write on the highs and lows of living abroad. These fascinating accounts of lives spent abroad in the past 150 years are a true celebration of the mix of cultural experience that makes the modern Welsh woman.

ISBN: 9781-870206-63-1
£7.99

Dew on the Grass
by Eiluned Lewis

A Honno Classics title with a new introduction by Dr Katie Gramich

Set in the Welsh borders, this enchanting autobiographical novel vividly evokes the essence of childhood and a vanished way of life. The novel was first published in 1934 to great acclaim.

ISBN: 9781-870206-80-8
£8.99

Short story anthologies from Honno

Coming Up Roses
Edited by Caroline Oakley

Everything's coming up roses. But not all of those roses are beautiful are sweet smelling – some have a touch of frost. Our gardens reflect out lives, from the regimented to the artfully dishevelled, the pristine to the neglected, and this collection of bittersweet stories in its variety. Welsh women write about gardens: what they mean to them, what happens in them and where they take them…

ISBN: 9781-870206-93-8
£7.99

Safe World Gone
Edited by Patricia Duncker and Janet Thomas

What would it take to change your world? In this exciting diverse anthology with stories that are by turns funny, touching and scary, Welsh women authors explore the turning points that can change a woman's life forever.

ISBN: 9781-870206-77-8
£7.99

A View Across the Valley: Short stories by women from Wales c. 1850-1950
Edited by Jane Aaron

Stories reflecting the realities, dreams and personal images of Wales – from the industrial communities of the south to the hinterlands of the rural west. This rich and diverse collection discovers a lost tradition of English-language short story writing.

ISBN: 9781-870206-35-8
£7.95

About Honno

Honno Welsh Women's Press was set up in 1986 by a group of women who felt strongly that women in Wales needed wider opportunities to see their writing in print and to become involved in the publishing process. Our aim is to develop the writing talents of women in Wales, give them new and exciting opportunities to see their work published and often to give them their first 'break' as a writer.

Honno is registered as a community co-operative. Any profit that Honno makes goes towards the cost of future publications. To buy shares or to receive further information about forthcoming publications, please write to Honno at the address below, or visit our website: **www.honno.co.uk**.

Honno
'Ailsa Craig'
Heol y Cawl
Dinas Powys
Bro Morgannwg
CF64 4AH

All Honno titles can be ordered online at www.honno.co.uk
or by sending a cheque to
Honno, MyW, Vulcan St, Aberystwyth. SY23 1JH
FREE p&p to all UK addresses